Vibrational UPgrade
A Conspiracy for Your Bliss

Vibrational UPgrade
A Conspiracy for Your Bliss

Easing Humanity's Evolutionary Transition

By Alison J. Kay, PhD

Copyright © 2016 Alison J. Kay, PhD

All rights reserved. No part of this book may be reproduced or transmitted in any form or by any means without written permission of the publisher, except in the case of brief quotations embodied in critical articles and reviews.

This material had been written and published solely for educational purposes. The author and the publisher shall have neither liability nor responsibility to any person or entity with respect to any loss, damage, or injury caused or alleged to be caused directly or indirectly by the information contained in this book.

The author of this book does not dispense medical advice or prescribe the use of any technique as a form of treatment for physical, emotional, or medical problems without the advice of a physician, either directly or indirectly. The intent of the author is only to offer information of a general nature to help you in your quest for wellbeing. In the event you use any of the information in this book for yourself or others, which is your constitutional right, the author and the publisher assume no responsibility for your actions.

ISBN: 978-0-9753668-0-6

Headshot in About the Author section
Zully A. Rosado Photography 2012

Babypie Publishing
Waitsfield, VT
www.BabypiePublishing.com

Table of Contents

Dedication	vii
Acknowledgments	ix
Introduction	xi
Preface	xvii

Beginner

Chapter One
    The Possibilities   23

Intermediate

Chapter Two
    We Take Ourselves So Seriously   45

Chapter Three
    The Subtle Is, Well, Subtle!   55

Chapter Four
    The Effects of Blocks and Chakras   87

Advanced

Chapter Five
    Replacing Forcing and Efforting with Allowing and Receiving   107

Chapter Six
    Allowing, Aligning, and Ananda   137

Chapter Seven
    Satyagraha: Love or Soul Force   157

Chapter Eight
    Turiya: The Fourth State of Consciousness   171

Conclusion   203
Next Steps   207
About the Author   209

Dedication

This book is dedicated to all the pioneers out there willing to take risks by stepping out of the status quo. For those who have the courage to follow their own inner GPS, trusting this universe's loving support for us and choosing to create their lives from this love, joy, and trust. We are leading the way into the new paradigm on behalf of all humanity during this time so ripe for change.

Thank you for being this vibration of choosing joy and freedom proactively, rather than needing crisis to demand it. It is providing a huge assist for us all during humanity's greatest leap in evolution, as these times are touted to be! Thank you for lovingly recognizing this about yourself—you are a potent creator! With more of us choosing these higher vibrations, the more accessible we make it for the masses, and the more we ensure a softer, smoother collective transformation.

Love!

Acknowledgments

Thank you to my dad, my brothers, and my cousins for the love and fortitude in reassembling our family based on the love with which Mom and Dad raised us.

I'd like to thank all of you who have helped me along the way become who I am—you know who you are.

I'd also like to thank all my clients, students, subscribers, and audiences from around the globe for your courage, your trust in me, your willingness to reach beyond the status quo, asking for more for your life, and for your beautiful expressions of gratitude to me! Your success is mine, and this book is what it is because of our work together.

Introduction

You are receiving a Vibrational UPgrade just from reading this book. Interwoven within all of the words themselves and the concepts presented is a super-charged set of frequencies, energies transmitted to your consciousness through mine as I wrote these words. You likely won't consciously recognize this—although some of you will! As you read, you will begin to notice changes and shifts in your thinking, what you pay attention to, your perspective, your new choices available, and hence in your behaviors and ultimately in your lives.

Welcome to your new life! We are here to be happy, live in joy, spread and receive and grow love and ourselves. This book is written for this purpose—and to ease it up for us all.

Because as I ask with the very title of my first book: *What If There's Nothing Wrong?*

What would we then create?

This is a magical time on our planet right now—the biggest shift in humanity's evolution.

What choices can we make that will make this transition full of ease?

What can we do to be enjoying this shift more?

Have fun and be love!

Many blessings to each and every one of us as we continue to awaken to our interconnectedness and oneness. We are transitioning into a new paradigm and life, collectively, based more on the energies of our hearts and less on the energies of our ego-minds. We continue to grow in our abilities to listen to and tend to the soils of our inner worlds and then create our outer worlds with more deliberation and inspiration.

And so it is!

You'll experience this throughout reading this book—little patches of the universe making themselves more known to you.

As I'm completing the book, I'm sitting at my local teahouse. The music really caught my attention today, because it was just one song, with one word, repeated over and over. It was stuck on play and repeat. My friend, who makes my unsweetened organic green tea day in and day out, told me they couldn't get it off repeat "for some strange reason."

The word?

"Desire."

Rather than overlooking this—because of a busy mind or a busy world with lots to get done, or writing it off as coincidence—I'm choosing to see it for what it is.

Is it desire that moves energy toward our creations?

Or is it the strength of our desire, emanating from our hearts that is the key to creativity?

Is this what gives us the power and ability to collapse waves into particles and create our reality, transforming invisible subtle energies into a tangible physicality, what we identify as reality?

And is it when we have a desire to fully create our lives, with all of its various components, that desire moves in to match the co-creative energy all around us—more than if it's just a cerebral plan?

This movement of energy is further brought into place as we actively choose, based on our desires, and thus go about the act of creating our lives one choice at a time. And it continues: desire, choice, allow, choose again, new desires, assess, allow for more, choose more. The constant expansion by those living on our planet right now is based on the co-creative abilities being called forward in each of us.

Is our being aware of our aligned desires and building our lives based on this enthusiastic energy one of the keys to creating what we desire with ease?

So what can we each be and do to have more clarity about what we're desiring and creating?

And then to choose based on our innermost desires?

And can we, allow ourselves to step beyond anything our mind is already familiar with creating as we reach into the unknown, allowing ourselves to even welcome the unknown as the sign of change that it is?

And what can we each do to birth this new world and have it show up in ways that are better than anything we ever could have imagined?

As I wrote this last line, a redheaded woodpecker flew overhead. I am not making this up! People who know me know this is the way it is in my world. A woodpecker symbolizes a new beat, a new rhythm, being drummed into our lives.

And so it is!

At birth all people are soft and yielding.
At death they are hard and stiff.
All green plants are tender and yielding.
At death they are brittle and dry.
When hard and rigid,
We consort with death.
When soft and flexible,
We affirm greater life.
~ Tao Te Ching 76

Preface

The times in which we live are considered humanity's greatest evolutionary leap forward.

What does it mean to have one's system reacting to these times in which we're living?

In the list below, it's likely you will recognize yourself in at least three of the descriptions. This shift really is happening—with very real effects in our lives.

- You've been told you're too sensitive.

- You've been told you're a seeker.

- You have always gone beyond and around the masses, building your life differently.

- You are aware that something is restless within you, and rather than checking out with distractions, you want to check into this restlessness, which is awakened energy.

- You've had a life event that has opened you up to look for the meaning of life.

- You've suffered the loss of a loved one and, out of desire to retain that connection, have reached beyond the physical plane to understand and connect and make sure he or she is okay.

- You have suffered the loss of a loved one and are looking for ways to connect with something bigger than your pain, giving meaning to your suffering and life.

- You have received a diagnosis and want to connect with something bigger than your diagnosis.

- You have had a life event—such as a near-death experience or a stupendous series of synchronicities where everything magically just seemed to come together, as if you're the center of the universe—and this has cracked you open to seek more of what this force is.

- You've seen how boring the average existence can be, and you're looking to live a life with more fun, meaning, and fulfillment.

- Internally and intuitively, you *know* something BIG is going on right now on our planet, and you're seeking to find out what this is and your role in it.

- You want to understand how to use what you sense are your innate gifts to help others live better lives in some way.

- You've experienced a life-altering event that ripped you open—a crisis—and you now want to choose more for yourself and your life.

- You're aware that the current paradigm—or reality—is limited, focused on pain, suffering, and lack, and you know this isn't the way it is and this doesn't work for you.

- You're seeking more richness in your everyday existence through a connection to Source, with more synchronicities, magic, and ease in creating a seemingly charmed life.

- You've been on your spiritual path forever, and you desire to have more energy supporting you now as you awaken and enlighten even more.

- You've been working with your mind, through meditation and mindfulness, and desire some further guidance through your practice.

- You've been engaged with creating your Observer of your life, thoughts, beliefs, behaviors, and choices, and desire more support to do this with more ease.

- You want to know the payoff to all of this work on the spiritual path.

- You desire to be lighter and filled with more life.

- You desire to have access to all that you are and be and move beyond any previous limitations.

- You want to realize your full potential as a human being.

Beginner

Chapter One

The Possibilities

All that we are is the result of what we have thought. We are formed and molded by our thoughts. Those whose minds are shaped by selfish thoughts cause misery when they speak or act. Sorrow rolls over them as the wheel of a cart follows the hooves of the bullock that draws it.

All that we are is the result of what we have thought: we are formed and molded by our thoughts. Those whose minds are shaped by selfless thoughts give joy when they speak or act. Joy follows them like a shadow that never leaves them.

~ Buddha

It's funny, maybe not in that ha-ha way, but more cosmic-irony funny. I've taught meditation for twenty-two years to folks of all ages, cultures, and genders from around the globe. Americans have their own particular way of construing meditation, for sure. But for any post-modernized, globalized citizen on planet Earth, it seems like there is this funny construction of meaning as to what meditation is, what should happen during meditation, and what it is meant to deliver.

The bottom line, though, is that it seems like all the noise the mind creates about meditation comes from its supposedly accurate conclusions that meditation is meant to *stop* — in no uncertain terms — us from looking within our own minds.

This is in part due to the relatively predominant human fear that there is some boogey man lurking in the back of our minds who wants to get us, so it's best not to go too deeply in there, nor really look in there at all. It creates a sense of running away from ourselves and shows up in all sorts of behaviors. These include shopping and buying things to affect a new consciousness around ourselves rather than grow ourselves into a new consciousness, not allowing ourselves to be alone or still, not getting too close to folks, not speaking to what is really on our minds — basically anything we do to avoid facing ourselves. Facing ourselves seems so serious and has implied explosions and eruptions for many. Yet the clamoring for alignment with our authentic selves seems to be pointing to doing exactly this.

This has its own unique tone, depending on cultural and religious backgrounds. For example, I've found my clients with a Catholic background — no matter the culture — have a texture to their beliefs about allowing their intuition to come forth that is tinged with a fear of punishment mixed with shame and guilt. They believe that if they were to open up their minds, looking beyond the everyday mind and its thoughts and beliefs that remain relatively stable, and into the part of them that is aware or intuitive or knowing or psychic, they'll get in trouble. Not only that, but it'll be dastardly trouble. In fact, that's why so many folks leave their beliefs intact and unexplored — in order to have some sense of stability, especially in today's world of such rapid change. So I've had a type of clearing and coaching style organically develop with my Catholic clients that contains reassurance and clears out any traumas of what may have happened in the past when they let themselves embody their own knowing and their power.

Power: some schools of thought, like access consciousness, call it *potency*. Maslow's hierarchy of needs in the Humanistic School of Psychology called it *self-actualization*. Still others in the yogic community refer to it as *kundalini*, while others in this same community call it *enlightenment*. And coming out of the yogic community and overlapping with the meditation and contemplative practices of the Buddhist community, it can also be referred to as *samadhi*, or *the bliss state*. This is where we have access to expanded consciousness, and thus our intuition can access the knowing of various things that are able to come through this channel developed through a quieted, disciplined mind. A quieted ego-mind can be made serviceable through the practice of meditation.

It's always interesting for me to observe the reaction in Western audiences when I am presenting my first signature talk and now a product on my website, "The Nature of the Mind." The Yogic teachings include eight limbs and the *asanas*, or body postures, we do in yoga are only one of the eight limbs of the spectrum of teachings Yoga offers. Working with the mind makes up five of the eight limbs.

And then, at a much more advanced level on the path of cultivating consciousness, after the ego-mind has been rendered serviceable — the "judge" of the ego-mind has been fired, and the witness of the more neutral consciousness and Awakened Presence has been hired — there is the fourth state of consciousness, *turiya*. In this context of turiya, the first three states of consciousness are considered to be waking, sleeping, and dreaming. Turiya — as presented to me from one of our main gurus bringing yoga to the United States, beloved Gurudev Yogi Desai — is the fourth state of consciousness. It is represented by the "OM" symbol. Turiya lies behind all of life and all the previous three states of consciousness — waking, sleeping, and dreaming. The more practices we engage in to render the ego-mind and its busy conclusions, judgments, and evaluations serviceable to our overall mind-body-spirit system, the more we advance toward experiencing this fourth state of consciousness and the more we can seamlessly weave it into our more conscious awareness.

About twenty-five years ago, I commanded: "Universe, help me increase my tolerance for bliss!"

What was behind that, in part, was a deep knowing that we are not meant to suffer. Nor are we here to be put through grueling tests so that our souls grow. And progressively, I've been led over the past twenty-five years to the teachings that contain this very same knowing. These new times we're living in—touted as the greatest shift in humanity's evolution, Humanity's Spiritual Awakening—have increasingly revealed to me that this greatly involves becoming much more consciously aware of our active roles as co-creators of our lives through our choices, day in and day out. It's not some mystical choice made in a moment of epiphany while meditating in a cave or on a vision quest or journeying on a shamanic journey in the desert, although in these times it can and does include this, in part for many removed from society. Our choices—at the mundane levels of our daily lives, marrying the sacred to the mundane at these very physical, task-oriented levels—weave into our existence the sacred.

The last description of turiya seems the closest to what it is that wants to be explored and expressed here. Yes, I've taught meditation countless times now, taking more new folks than I can count through the process of developing a stabilized practice and cultivating mindfulness and the awakened presence behind their eyes to apply to their daily lives, at the level where our moment-to-moment choices are made. And most recently, after numerous requests, I have finally acquiesced and began teaching my own energy medicine, the Vibrational UPgrade System.

My Vibrational UPgrade System (VUPS) is based on what I know about where one can go within the energies that we access more easily when we're not coming from the everyday thinking, easily distracted, attached mind. Some, if not much of this, is how to connect with that fourth level of consciousness, turiya, for creating a life that goes far beyond just surviving, to thriving. It's not a linear process, where we have to do it step-by-step. It's just a clean way to communicate it to our minds.

It does seem, though, that first we have to have moved through the first major, life-changing "*Aha!*" of recognizing that we are not our minds' thoughts. This then, if built upon, leads to more detachment from that Judging Mind and Reactive Mind and to more of the neutral Awakened Presence. We eventually have enough experiences applying this to life that we are successful at not being triggered when the mind tell us to react. Reactivity seems to happen when we are locked into survival mode—the work-obligations-family-tasks cycle—typically operating, therefore, with unexamined, habitual, subconscious patterns.

Yet when we are able to maintain mindfulness during a typically difficult interaction—let's say traffic and we have been known to get enraged when cut off—and we do not react a few times in a row when cut off, then this shows us *experientially* that we don't have to believe our thoughts. This growth has to be experienced; it can't be taught to the linear mind as factual information. It's a dance between this information, practice, experiences, and then gaining more information, more practice, more experiences, and more expansion. In fact, just today I had a client, also a student of my Vibrational UPgrade energy medicine, who told me about having this precise experience for the first time in traffic, hence the freshness of that example. As a result, she has awakened to some of what else is possible when she aligns more with the sacred in her mundane life, beyond the everyday mind and its habitual thought patterns and triggers, locked into the survival mode of living that the majority are still engaged within. However, you are different if you are reading these words. You have come to a point where you're sensing, at least, if not knowing, that something else is possible, and something else is going on.

In other words, once we come out of our lifelong personalities that everyone has told us we are, this becomes more possible. Preferably it's by choice, and not a forcing of circumstances that causes us to move beyond this basic level of life. And once we rise above, or go beyond the beliefs, conclusions, judgments, and perceptions that our minds are firing away all the time about who we need to be, who we should not be, what we need to do to feel good and have pleasure, and what we need to avoid to continue that pleasure and not feel pain—this is what I'm talking about: the liberation that comes from no longer being locked into what we have always listened to—our minds' interpretation of all of life, and its perceptions of who did what and who didn't do what, and what something is and isn't—yields new experiences with changed outcomes to those everyday, normal situations. This gets people hooked on this new path.

Just today I had a student ask on one of my calls during my *Your Sensitivity Is Your Power* telecall series, "I know more is going on, but how do I make that a part of *this* reality everyone else is operating within?"

What I've just explained is the beginning of an answer to this very poignant question. It is not some lofty, high ideal. It is a marriage of the sacred and mundane, weaving the sacred into our everyday, mundane lives via the choices we make from an illuminated, Awakened Presence.

Until then, there's that dog-chasing-its-tail sense of staying locked into a thought-dominated existence. The mind, with its thoughts and conclusions, decides it doesn't want to meditate and determines meditation is stupid, useless, a waste of time, too difficult, or whatever else the mind has to say to ensure that we do not go near meditation, meaning that we do not go near the mind. Further, this keeps us from questioning the very hidden, subconscious beliefs that have us locked into making the same old choices, unconsciously, day in and day out, and closing off to life instead of increasingly opening and expanding.

Visualize the biggest tree you know, perhaps a southern oak, as opposed to a giant redwood — meaning one with more branches that are reaching out, extending beyond the trunk. That visual gives a sense of what I'm talking about. That is expansion and it is the nature of all life.

Meditation is just getting to know our minds. This leads us, eventually, if continuing the process of living an examined life, to see how our hidden beliefs and conclusions keep us locked into unconscious, robotic living. Much of this can be based around thoughts and beliefs that our minds tell us that aren't even true. For example, one can be both wealthy and a good person, instead of the hidden conclusion that I've observed from many — that those who are wealthy as greedy and therefore bad people. Or they believe they got wealthy by being bad people. And so, if people with this hidden conclusion are having a challenging time financially, then perhaps this subconscious belief is blocking them from allowing themselves to have wealth because they didn't want to be bad people. Having this understanding of their hidden beliefs would help them close the gap between what they say they want and even what they're actively going for, but not getting the results they consciously say they desire.

In knowing one's mind, one has gained the edge in observing all the distasteful thoughts the mind can and does churn out. And this includes being able to simply see what absolute shite the mind can turn out! This is also true for subconscious and unconscious thoughts. Although at this level, when looking below the conscious mind's thoughts with the work I do clearing blocks and guiding folks to and through their subconscious and unconscious beliefs, it's fun to observe the absolute inanity and insanity of a thought. That childlike subconscious makes most of these seemingly inane conclusions from the perspective of a child learning how to do life on planet Earth at the most basic level—in response to asking one's self: *How do I get love and food?*—so these beliefs do tend to be quite illogical but can be really cute. So if a child is trying to form an understanding of how to get that display of affection from his dad that makes him feel so warm and fuzzy, and the child observes that Dad seems to give it to Mom when she smiles and listens and nods and doesn't interrupt, then the child is likely to conclude that this is what he should do to also get that feeling of love and approval.

This happens during the formative years of ages two to eight, when the neurological wiring is being created. This gets wired in at a subconscious level, as if a command that this is then how to do life when seeking that loving feeling.

The childlike innocence would then carry this over to how to be in other social settings, because that is the rudimentary level our subconscious works at. It helps us perform functions of survival. If you think of driving a car, when first learning it was conscious involvement and processing. Then, once the skill is consciously learned, it gets bumped down to the subconscious level of functions and tasks needed for survival.

The gig we're talking about here, though, is the multiplying effects this has in that child's conclusions about communication and love and approval, bleeding the effects of this conclusion into other arenas, and showing up in behaviors that at some point become self-restricting. Overall, within meditation alone, before clearing subconscious and unconscious beliefs that aren't really true and serve as blocks to expansion, the practice of pulling up and off the thoughts whenever one is able to *Observe*—and here I use a capital "O" to indicate that this is the work of the Observer—that one is thinking creates more space. More distance is felt between who we are and who these thoughts tell us we are, so that gradually the importance of the mind and its thoughts deflates.

Again, that is why the mind, with its judgments, absolutely tries to keep us away from meditating. Once we do it anyway and have cultivated a certain amount of space and detachment, making the mind and its thoughts significant is no longer as much of a hidden agreement and we no longer allow the mind to rule our lives. Instead, choice becomes available, both choice in what thoughts we choose to pay attention to later, after meditation, and choice in what thoughts to simply ignore. This happens over time, after the musculature gets a chance to develop from repeated efforts, as if lifting weights for bicep curls in a gym. It results in having enough rehearsed detaching from the mind's thoughts—no matter the content during meditation—to then become available during all of life, save for dreaming. That just requires more advancement in working with our consciousness.

That's what I'm talking about. We live in such a mind-dominant world, that to consider there is life that exists beyond what our typical thoughts have us locked into as our lifestyles requires pioneers, special people with enough courage to look within. It is such an exquisitely brave act to look within our own gardens and trash heaps that the mind's thought factory is. It requires such bravery to allow ourselves to see what the smaller self is doing in its game of playing it safe and hiding behind its assumed status quo.

That is the game of survival that happens when we operate from a lack consciousness: there isn't enough time, money, energy, or happiness, and we must strive to get more at all times. There is no space nor time nor need to do anything beyond this, because this is what we see others doing, and all that we do is what we see others doing. This is what we do. And this has been the dominant paradigm for quite a long time now, and it has served societies well.

So this is the act of getting to know our minds and their typical thoughts. And then the insights that come from this create the musculature to gradually not be enslaved to our thoughts. And this is when it really gets *fun*!

But before we move on, it is important to consider this: where did we get the thoughts we find our minds conditioned with?

Who started this societal structure anyway?

Who started, in America for example, to stress the importance of being active and productive rather than active and then passive, say with the type of siesta time most cultures around the planet have made part of their daily foundation?

I remember Chinese colleagues of mine, when I taught at an international school in Asia, pulling pillows out of their desks to put their heads down in that afternoon lull time.

Pillows at work?

And then using them and letting others see?

Wow, was my American mind enthralled and horrified!

My entire first book of 416 pages, *What If There's Nothing Wrong?* explores how our typical thoughts become conditioned and what we think about, choose, and live; so we won't explore that here. I just mention it as a reminder, that when we're cleaning out our minds' clutter, much of it isn't even ours to begin with.

Let's look at the next stage of what we access once we've gained the footing of not believing every thought our minds have, and having created space from an engaged practice that grows this space.

Who are we, then, when we have a gap of a second in between our thinking mind's thoughts?

Who are we, really, if we can train ourselves to let go of a thought and examine our thinking minds at work?

Doesn't that imply that we are more than our thinking minds and therefore thoughts?

Who is then Observing the thinking mind, labeled in this field's lingo as the Observer, or the Witness, the Witnessing Presence, or Presence?

This is where it gets *fun* indeed! Now we've lightened up in many different ways and aren't taking ourselves quite so seriously anymore. I know what I already know is possible. And I've already seen in my own life what becomes possible once we allow ourselves to be more of an open receiving station, which is within our natural wiring throughout our system's happy, singing cells.

I have witnessed what I have access to when I'm playing with my own consciousness and its connection to all that is. I can speak of the massive availability of immensely supportive, loving, joyous juice and vitality, and levels of creativity that were barely considered possible. Once I've cultivated my receptivity and alignment out of the thinking mind and its influences from the masses who are still in fear, it is able to roam free and connect and align and create and choose and direct my life based on this connection to my Source and source energy. *The Source* is however we construe that bigger pool of information that comes in from the area or parts of us and our consciousness that are not in the locked-down mode of survival-based living, doing what everyone else is.

I know when I teach my clients, students, and audiences what then becomes available. And I do this through the road map of the chakra system. The chakra system is brilliant in the way it can capture all aspects of life and how it affects our lives, choices, bodies, and relationships based on its ancient and reliable wisdom of how and where our minds, bodies, and spirits intersect.

Whenever I've presented this information to an audience, at least three-quarters if not all the participants thump back into their seats and say, "No way! That's me! I have those exact issues!"

Some have said this out loud. This occurs while they listen to me go through the list for each of the chakras of its physical, mental, emotional, and bodily impacts on our lives and thus what issues this creates when any of the seven main chakras are out of balance. When I go through this list—and usually I'm only on the third of the seven chakras—people begin to see the challenges in their lives reframed, with a new, holistic understanding that is helpful guidance to them on how to become issue-free. This list of aspects is on my website in brief, with the *Chakra Attunement* audio series, so you can see for yourself and have this same experience.

I discuss that list in this book less systematically, more in the form of providing concrete examples from my clients and students. In this way, you can glean the absolute supreme intelligence behind our human design that is entirely unable to be overlooked once self-examination is applied in response to this information. Indeed, knowing what I know—and seeing what I've seen from the lens of letting the chakras guide me as I work with people and have worked with myself, and ultimately seeing how all can be unraveled should a person choose this—has given me solid embodiment of my knowing there is a Source bigger than us all who created our systems to be such elegant examples of love put forth into a human mind-body-spirit system.

This vast, wise compilation of information put forth from the yogic sages will cause revelations in you consistent with the thousands who already have had the experience described above. Their experiences served as their road map for insight into their own larger systems of consciousness that contains conscious, subconscious, and unconscious levels. Yet beyond that, it seems something more wants to come through me, causing me to write this book now.

Today we sit on the precipice of what this "something more" is. I was at the Mayan ruins for the December 21, 2012 Galactic Alignment. That's a rather big term, *Galactic Alignment.* Sounds important. And it seems as if it is. I was the yoga and meditation teacher and energy medicine practitioner for a group of advanced scientists, scholars, and practitioners with varying aspects of our mind-body-spirit system and humanity's evolution as their focus. There was a special arrangement made to have a ceremony with a Mayan shaman at the Mayan pyramids, where their calendar, which predicted the importance of 2012, was devised.

Now, I have a special connection, apparently, which I wasn't quite so consciously aware of at the time of these events. Some of that can be witnessed through the choice that was given to me when asked to host a show on the Internet's largest online media outlet around the myths of what 2012 meant, so that people could feel more aligned with the actual significance, if any, of this time on our planet. So for two years and three months around—both before and after—this date that the Mayans and other cultures had predicted, I hosted many specialists on my radio show discussing the nature of the times we were living in. This included many of the scientists I quote in my first book, *What if There's Nothing Wrong?* who have been pioneers in scientifically measuring consciousness, meditation, and subtle energies. This also included my own knowing, as I continued to ask questions of the universe about the significance of the times we're living in, and listened to my inner guidance's responses, continuing to increasingly open up with more receptivity, asking to gain more awareness so I could better help.

So there we were, this special group of us, at the Mayan pyramids on 12/21/12. We were told to wear all white. Our group was broadcasted on international and national television, as I came to find out later from friends as far as Poland who saw a shot of me there at the pyramids. I reflected on the fact that the Mayan ruins were the very first place I flew to internationally following my return to the States after living in Asia for ten years. At that time, I had taken a friend with me to Cancun, wanting to visit the Mayan ruins, but not really knowing why. The understanding of the significance of 12/21/12 and my role in it wasn't totally conscious then. I was not doing the radio show yet. We went to Chichen Itza, the very same site I returned to on 12/21/12, but there were no film crews dotting the area where we toured that year before the alignment.

But that second time, a year-and-a-half later on 12/21/12, I was there in all-white with my bare feet, feeling like there was some electrical pulsing machine attached to them underneath, because that ground was full on surging with electricity. And there were film crews all over. I barely noticed them because we were caught up in the ceremony with the elder male Mayan shaman telling us that when the Mayans built the pyramids 2,000 years ago, they built them in those shapes pointing to the sky to assist the Earth in being able to *harness* the high vibrations they saw would be pouring down onto it during these times of the Galactic Alignment of 12/21/12. No ifs, ands, or buts about it; there were going to be some *high* frequencies showering down onto the Earth. And in order for the Earth to not burn up, they saw the need to structure these rocks in pyramids pointing toward the heavens. Perhaps, as I am wondering now because the Mayan shaman did not mention this, they were also built to help the Earth *make good use of* these high frequencies for her benefit. It reminds me of the kundalini energy spoken of in the yogic and Tibetan tantric worlds. The initial bolt of energy released begins the awakening process.

The lovely Mayan shaman said something else that has really stayed with me and recently has been more prominent in my consciousness. He said that these frequencies were seen to bring in such changes to humanity that it wouldn't be clear for three years if humanity was going to be able to handle and make good use of these frequencies, or burn itself up, so to speak, due to the upgrades these high frequencies would command within the human system.

What has also been said by others since 2012's Galactic Alignment is that 2015 is the year of the physical manifestation of what was seeded within consciousness around the 12/21/12 energetic influx. And, even more specifically, that September through November were going to be key in seeing the effects of what these high frequencies have been moving humanity toward. This is when I chose to write this book.

One more thing here: this Galactic Alignment of 12/21/12 can be termed however you want. What seems to be the repeated terminology describing this time on planet Earth, let's say from approximately 2010 to 2015, is that it is humanity's greatest leap in evolution ever, and that it is our Spiritual Awakening, both collectively and individually.

Now you can allow your mind to judge and push away and separate from what is being brought forth here, based on how out there or woo-woo you think these terms sound. I tend to address these ego-mind protests by looking at how both the yogic and Taoist paths are very much steeped in the basic understanding of the macrocosm being reflected in the microcosm. They have created many life-sustaining and life-promoting practices based on this.

Or you can choose to allow those thoughts, judgments, and labels to pass by — because it's the mind doing what the mind does — and open further to receive the possibilities being suggested here.

What is it that is coming in now at the close of 2015?

I am not clear about it as of yet, but it seems as huge as what blasted onto our planet in December 2012. What others who are not fear-based are saying is that a whole new potential of our abilities within the subtle energy realms is coming, to be made available to the masses. Another way to explain this is the yogi masters and monks who can do some pretty fantastic feats with energy that seem like it's a part of their everyday lives. Maybe all this is being opened up within all of humanity. Another description of what is going on now is that more of our DNA is becoming activated for a higher, more advanced evolution.

What I do know is that I have been listening and then following the information coming through as my guidance. This has been as far reaching as where to take my life, and how to assist clients in transforming what they've come to me to transform, and then everything in between, around, under, and above that.

If I were to Observe what my choices have been, based on the inner guidance I received when I asked questions, it would seem that indeed, I have been being asked to assist folks in surpassing this lower version of themselves. This lower version is where all the heavy beliefs and negative conditioning are that weigh us down and make us choose not to be open to life. This shutdown has caused a condition in their lives that has reached a point such that they're coming to me, seeking relief from this condition. And a great portion of my clients also come to me so that they can be even more open than they are, making advancements on their spiritual paths—awakened, activated, and open to even more brilliance in their lives.

But no matter the condition, really what I seem to have been doing for the past five years is opening up people's systems to something greater. Since being back in the States, I've been doing this work full time and full on, as opposed to the part-time work I had while teaching and being an administrator within the international school system and studying subtle energy at its source in Asia.

What does this something greater look like?

Well, ultimately from my working within my own and my clients' systems, and my guidance and their systems' guidance, what has become closed down is shown to me. I then send consciousness, or light, or information into this area. The way I deliver this is not to just attend to the closed-down area, or issue, or chakra, *but to open up all of their system*. Then it becomes a fully functioning, flowing chakra system as it supports health, vitality, well-being, creativity, spiritual connection, intuitive guidance, courage to take risks, increased connection with others, increased compassion and forgiveness, increased self-empowerment to create in the world what it is that we really desire, rather than what we just accept as all we're meant to have; or, in other words, rather than settling.

This balance brings full receptivity and openness and connection to what our feelings are really telling us. The balance brings full-on engagement with the sensual in life. And it all comes with a rooted, grounded, stabilized embodiment of this vast system of consciousness. It feels like it wants to be here in the body, on planet Earth, and fully welcomed, wanted, loved, and supported to be able to create an awakened life from the awakened, vital life-force energy surging throughout our systems. Whew!

Huge, right?

It's way, way beyond just survival or just getting by or just powering through.

What this also does, frankly, is raise our vibrations. Over and over again, clearing a client's system includes clearing each chakra's congested energy that hasn't had a chance to get balanced from daily living, but also the historical, foundational energy patterns that run a person at an unconscious level. When I go in with this light, or energy, it liberates the deadened, trapped, congested unconsciousness into more consciousness that can then join the party of happy cells singing joyous, vibrant health and love songs throughout a person's system.

That may sound whacked, but it's what I'm doing! And perhaps the level of wackiness that this is perceived with is indicative of how much we've been entrained to limitation, rather than unlimited possibilities.

The single most frequent comment I hear from clients—whether they came to me for spiritual awakening; depression or excessive worrying; wanting to get over their lack of consciousness and money issues; wanting a more alive, less robotic life than their corporate jobs provide; chronic pain; or even relief from digestive upset—if they keep working with me for the course, then inevitably comes the proclamation: "I haven't felt like this since I was a kid!"

Something is being asked to come alive. You are sensing it; otherwise there's no way you'd be this far into this book.

But for the masses, for all of us, for all of humanity, you are the pilgrims on the forefront leading the way, going beyond your mind's habitual thoughts and factory of thinking, and with your raised vibration, elevated beyond the drudgery of everyday, mundane living you're seeking, sensing, and asking, "What else is possible?"

Instead of living a drab, shutdown, checked-out existence day to day, just getting by, you're learning how to bring the magic, the sacred, that charged energy right there, smack dab into your everyday, mundane living. And the mastery of becoming fully the co-creators of our sacred lives that we are meant to live begins at the mundane level. Here's to our collective Awakening!

Intermediate

Chapter Two

We Take Ourselves So Seriously

Nothing kills the ego like playfulness, like laughter. When you start taking life as fun, the ego has to die; it cannot exist anymore.

~ Osho

The more we're locked into our thinking minds, the more seriously we take ourselves. The mind has a job to do: stuff to figure out, problems to fix, and issues to take care of. One of the main functions of our linear mind is to problem-solve. It has been given to us as a part of our human system in order to protect us. Some of the oldest biological wiring we have that is a part of this protective mechanism of our ego-mind is the fight-or-flight mechanism. This is wired into us to warn us of danger in our external environment. If something is a threat or there is a possible danger, then our minds register this at a very old, deep level and off goes the signaling to our adrenals to release hormones that are essential to our response to a perceived threat.

It is interesting to me that when I am giving wellness mini-sessions at expos, festivals, and events, I have come to notice that what people's systems are asking for is for me to hold my hands at the base of the brainstem. This seems to be communicating to me that there is something going on, especially when it is seven out of eight of the people on my table in one day, if not all. And what this seems to represent is that there is something with the oldest part of our brain that the majority need some light to get to, or energy, or *chi*, or life force, or information. When I asked my guidance what this was about, I heard that it is part of the massive shift going on within us now, in this biggest leap in humanity's history. It is our spiritual awakening. And this basic part of the brain that contains the fight-or-flight mechanism may be being upgraded into something more needed in this new era.

It may mean, too, that perhaps the mechanism within us that has been given the job of alerting us to danger and automatically turning on our body's ability to have more access to energy to fight or go into flight is outdated. Maybe this severe of a warning of danger is no longer needed, seeing as few of us still interact with lions, tigers, and bears.

So what is this protection mechanism in our ego-mind anyway?

The ego-mind's job is to protect us; we've already established that. It's a wonderful design; we have something within us that naturally communicates *and* sets up our systems to deal with danger. But although these big sources of physical danger are no longer as relevant, we still have the wiring. So instead of being applied to the wild and alerting us to step around that poisonous snake and to look behind us as the wolf approaches the path we're walking on, it is alerted to our everyday lives in suburban or urban or rural living. Now sure, when living in a city, learning to look over our shoulders and be alert to our surroundings is necessary, especially when a female, alone, in a city at night walking down a street.

I remember being in Old Town, Virginia and walking down the sidewalk by all the pubs, cafes, and shops on a Saturday night when I was there for my first book tour. All that could be heard was the click of my boot heels on the sidewalk. As a man approached me, I looked to the other side of the street to see if anyone was there to help me should he try something. Then I turned my eyes back to him and put my tuners on him to assess if he was a threat, and I got that he wasn't. Still, I wanted to be more comfortable, so I crossed the street.

As I did, he called after me, "Man, those heels sound sexy," as he walked toward the pubs and I to my hotel to work out in the fitness center that was, thankfully, in alignment with my schedule and open twenty-four hours.

So yes, there are still threats in which our most basic instinctual wiring, in conjunction with our ego-mind, support us in our safety. But really, overall, it has nothing to focus on, so it's in overdrive and assessing threats and dangers where there are none. For example, we see a police car and we've doing nothing wrong, but we still worry as the police car is on the side of the road.

"Will he or she bust us for speeding?" asks the mind, even as we look down at the speedometer and see that we're going only five miles over the speed limit and aren't in danger of getting pulled over.

Or our husband or kids or wife or partner hasn't called when they said they were going to call and *bam*! Off our minds go.

Is something wrong with the children? Are they hurt?

Is my partner out with someone else?

Is my spouse keeping secrets from me?

And on and on the mind goes, causing so much suffering.

This is the ego-mind's protective mechanism in overdrive. But it has good intentions: to keep us safe. However, as it sets about protecting us, it naturally looks for dangers and threats in the environment. And the way it works is to see problems. Frequently, with an untrained mind in today's times and especially if we're plugged into the news broadcasts or newspapers, we have a mind that goes quite easily into what I've come to term *runaway fear*. This runaway fear is not really justifiable; meaning, you really can't point to the actual source of the fear. Rather, you look for sources to blame for this fear. This feeling of unease is a restless mind looking for something to do.

It is a problem solver, and if there are no problems to solve, what does it then do?

Yes! It creates the problems.

American society, compared to many others, is one in which there is a focus on fixing problems. Openly voicing what one feels — due to freedom of speech and other unspoken agreements that come from having freedom of speech — creates this major vein within American society. And within a democracy that once encouraged civil action and participation in this democracy through freedom of speech and the right to assemble, as well as all the items on the Bill of Rights, there is a lot of open dialogue about identifying society's problems and ways to fix these problems. Now this is good, sure! It creates an open forum and a system of elected officials held responsible by the constituents who voted for them.

Add to this mix the prolific use of the Internet with chat rooms and social media — again, another great thing in concept and many uses of social media create positive change. One aspect that this has created is a forum where people can easily express all that is wrong. And if folks in their everyday lives are tired of hearing others complain, then the anonymity offered by social media provides a perfect forum for one to let it all out, without real repercussions. On a slightly different note, I was listening to an interview of a celebrity on a late-night show, and she was saying she secretly takes encouraging pictures from Instagram and puts them in a file on her laptop so she can look at them, but doesn't want to let people know she likes this kind of stuff due to fear of being seen as cheesy.

So is one main focus of social media creating a means for checking out, where what is favored is following celebrities, rather than what is positive and contributory to cultivating a more meaningful life?

It is obviously not the intention of this book to discuss social media and all its implications and effects on and within society. But it is to point out the increased opportunity for us to stay locked into voicing blame and pointing to sources outside ourselves for causing our suffering or problems. If and when social media is used in this way, it encourages the ego-mind to ignore what is real and good in our lives, and check in even deeper to what is wrong.

Add to this now something even further: the deadening of life force that the Wi-Fi and computer signals send off. They're not the biologically based life-force energies; they're artificial. And there is a deadening of the frequencies that this man-made technology has on the electro-magnetic biofield and chi of humans and the Earth. So if we spend a lot of time on the computer and within Wi-Fi frequencies without tending to our biofield, we are more easily locked into the same frequencies on that continuum of life-force-deadening frequencies of the ego-mind.

Simply put, spending time in an artificial environment without keeping this balanced with cultivation of one's life force energy — by going into nature, exercising, eating alive foods, interacting with other humans in an authentic, expressive way — enforces living life from the ego-mind, because it is also of the same type of life-force-deadening frequency as the laptop and Wi-Fi and cell phones we use often for social media.

This deadening of the life force that enhances the activation of the ego-mind keeps us in a cycle of being mind dominant.

When we live in this way, we could be described as "talking heads floating above bodies."

This visual is very much how many people who come to me and whom I teach feel, and they wonder why they feel like there's a gray cloud overwhelming their lives.

This dulling down of our life force results in less life juice, so to speak, bubbling up throughout our systems. That means we have less vibrant energy circulating throughout our systems. It also means that we will tend to be even more locked into our minds. It is a cycle. If we are used to exercising, then we're used to being in our bodies. Perhaps we also watch what we eat and make sure to feed the body what it wants in order to fuel the workouts and then recover from the workouts and to keep it in general tip-top shape. And the body becomes more appreciated when we ask it to perform athletic endeavors for us.

But when we are not circulating life force energy throughout our systems due to the demands of our work and we're living to work instead of working to live, or we're spending more time inside and less outside in touch with the natural part of life, or we have not tended to Observing and listening to our thoughts, or we're focused mostly on the external world, typically this creates fertile ground for the ego-mind to dominate.

And when it dominates, so does the lifelong personality we've always had projected onto us, and we live from this. So does the analytical mind and its desires to fix, problem-solve, analyze, figure out, and calculate. And when there isn't a task for the ego-mind, and it is used to running the show, it will create problems to fix, so it remains useful.

This is where we end up locked into living life from our minds, become talking heads, and take ourselves too seriously. Interestingly, within the chakra column, the sixth chakra is the one responsible for intuition. It is also the one we go to if we are taking our lives too seriously. Clear it of foundational energy patterns, and boost it to act at optimal and balanced levels. This does in fact include a rebalancing that occurs from taking ourselves and our lives too seriously.

I have seen many clients and students who have highly analytical jobs— accountants, scientists, project managers, marketing analysts, social media gurus, professors, attorneys, bank managers, CFOs, and more—and once we have their sixth chakra balanced, their tendency to take life so seriously dissipates tremendously.

The course of the other chakras I also work intensely contributes to this pattern at a secondary level and tends to vary from person to person. But it is always this sixth chakra that is our center for balanced hemispheric use and the seat of our intuition— and our sinus cavity—that gets congested the more we analyze and take things seriously, and the less we listen to our internal guidance. It is connected to a Higher Source from the chakra above it, the crown chakra.

We are not wired to be only the ego. It just seems that way because of how our society, globally now, has remained comfortable in going after the ego's pursuits. This does, of course, include a vast array of commercial activities. Yet we are seeing an increase in folks who are what is called today *heart-based entrepreneurs*. These people work toward a situation in which the economy created contributes to the well-being of a person's overall mind, body, and spiritual system, and to the Earth's sustainability.

Again, the ego is not bad. It is a necessary tool downloaded into our systems for useful purposes. Some of these purposes are now out of date, and it seems like our systems overall are indeed going through upgrades, perhaps including the rewiring of the fight-or-flight mechanism. It is just when we let it run out of control that we then think it's the only option available. And this brings us to the point where we don't recognize that we are able to actually choose which thoughts to listen to and act on from all the thoughts our ego-mind churns out. That is not good, because it causes us to misidentify and misalign with whom we really are, what life is really about, and what we're here for. Whatever we're here for, it seems that increasingly, more and more people than ever before are asking to find work that is more meaningful and provides them with a sense of fulfillment. And this, again, is the nature of our times.

A spiritual awakening involves awakening to the spirit in ourselves and all of life. This goes beyond the ego-mind. This is what we're currently doing, some of us with more grace and less pain and suffering than others.

What if the point in life is to feel good?

To have fun?

What if that is what activates our life force to awaken more than anything?

And what if the feeling of being on a sailboat brings that up for us because of the freedom felt?

Well, that's great! I am not saying to deny all ego desires. What I am saying is the misidentification of who we really are and staying locked in the unconsciousness and subconscious blocks are what I've seen over and over again that cause people's suffering, pain, and dis-ease. This has resulted from living as if that's all we are, without something really special being within each and every one of us that contributes to the good of the overall whole, which is us aligned with our own unique Being.

Forgetting who we are keeps us emphasizing things that are outside of us, in the external world, as if the external world is the most important. The physically tangible is what the ego is geared to help us navigate on and through, and if we're living from the ego, then we are focused on the physically tangible. And so, from my vantage point, a society full of people seeking to work to live and not live to work, and have work that leaves them feeling fulfilled rather than numbed down and empty, is the result of an ego-driven paradigm.

Many folks now in the West are asking for more in life than commercial pursuits. They're asking for *fun* while they earn a good living for themselves and their families that also contributes in some way to our global society. This is an awakened version; an awakened version to what is eternal and not temporary. The life force is alive and wants to expand through each of us. Living from within a body in which this is closed down has us not seeking expansion in these freedom-giving ways, but instead keeps us choosing more of what brings comfort—like the status quo—which comes from ego.

Do you see?

If you want a life that is more magical, that has more to it than just dulled-down energy where you're doing the same thing over and over again—mandates of the ego—then you have to reach for where the magic is. And this is beyond the everyday mind so heavily influenced by the ego, a.k.a. *the ego-mind*.

This is only one part of us. This is, in fact, only one part of our minds. It is the most obvious one, which was given to us to navigate everyday life on the physical plane with our five physical senses to make sense out of what our sensory organs pick up.

Why would we go to such a simplistic, mechanical tool used for labeling, judging, evaluating, concluding, analyzing, calculating, and keeping us safe from any incoming threats from anything new, when we want to live a life beyond what we've known so far?

If this is, in fact, Humanity's Spiritual Awakening, and it is humanity's greatest evolutionary leap, and people are looking for more meaning to their lives, and want to live in a healthier, more balanced and sustainable way—why would we go to the part of us that is not programmed for that?

It is our Higher Selves that see through our unconsciousness and subconscious blocks, formed erroneously from something not good that happened in our childhood years, to our perfection, and want to help our systems thrive with this sprouting fountain of expansive energy, our life force energy.

Wouldn't we go to that part of us and cultivate it?

Do you see?

Chapter Three

The Subtle Is, Well, Subtle!

Endurance is lost rapidly if one ceases to work at its maximum.

~ Bruce Lee

Don't ask yourself what the world needs, ask yourself what makes you come alive. And then go do that. Because what the world needs is people who have come alive.

~ Howard Thurman

What does it mean to be more in tune with the subtle energies in life?

We'll go through this with a few examples that reveal different levels of subtle energies, to ensure its applicability to your life. Please understand that I come from a perspective that was and is deeply affected by all my research and living in Asia for ten years conducting this research on subtle energy. So when I say, in a comparison-and-contrast type of statement, that in Asia they do something and here in the West, specifically the United States, we do something else, it is not to make what we do here bad or wrong. Instead, it is to move forward to being even more masterful within one's own system that is made up of subtle energy.

These subtle energies move and flow throughout our systems based on our beliefs. Beliefs are also subtle energy, as are feelings and emotions. Our level of vitality is also subtle energy. Our cravings, desires, repulsions, thoughts, beliefs, judgments, conclusions, projections, and decisions — all are thoughts and are all subtle energies. Each one has its own frequency, or vibration, attached to it. A happy thought and then feeling is one type of thought and feeling. A critical thought and the ensuing feeling of contraction or shutting down is another group of thoughts and seemingly uncontrollable feelings. A happy thought has a higher, lighter, and faster vibration than a critical one. Criticism and judgment have a heavier and slower vibration, or frequency.

All of life is broken down into frequencies and vibrations. This is known and acknowledged within some of the world's oldest and most illuminated cultures about the human design. Both Hebrew (Kabbalistic, to be more specific, which are the mystical teachings of Judaism, not taught in Hebrew school or what one learns before a Bat Mitzvah), and Hindu Indian Yogic, for example, teach that there is a sound the world started with, or the big bang started with. The word is *OM* for the Hindu Yogic world, and *Aleph* is the letter, with *A* being the sound that started the universe according to Kabbalistic, Hebrew thinking. This sound has one of the highest vibrations, if not the highest, in all of existence, likely because it is considered to have *started* existence. If we take a moment and look at the chakra system, the highest vibrating chakra at the top of the chakra column is the crown chakra, located at the crown of the head and associated with the OM tone. This chakra is the one within the chakra column that is thought to be the source for connection to Source energy, or divinity.

When citizens of any modernized, globalized culture rush around to get everything done we need to in order to raise families, create corporations, run businesses, and engage in life in this globalized, modernized way, there is an element of running along on the more physical, surface levels of life, depending on how busy we are. It seems our busy-ness is typically an indicator of how much we're engaged on the physical plane of life, without spending as much time on the more subtle planes, for example, of subtle energy. This does depend, however, on how much time we put into our schedules to slow down and connect with this part of existence and ourselves. This is not to say that if we lead busy, productive lives then we are automatically only existing and working on the physical plane of life. It is a question of being shown the value of spending time going within, and showing the value of paying attention to subtle energies. As it stands now, the physical and what is considered productive within the physical plane is valued in Western society; whereas thoughts, feelings, emotions, and awareness of energy are relegated to the backseat, comparatively speaking.

The value of the effects of the subtle energies in our lives has to exist in order to motivate us to choose to carve time out of our daily, busy lives. I moved to Asia specifically because I wanted to live within cultures that appreciated energy, understood energy, and could teach me their ancient secrets about the subtle energies. While living there, a part of me felt more at home due to this acknowledgement and understanding of subtle energies — or energy — that don't happen for me when living stateside, at least not yet.

This valuing of the subtle energies exists within the Chinese and Indian cultures more than it does in the West and, more specifically, in the United States. Both the Chinese and Hindu Indian cultures have medical systems based on holistic principles, which acknowledge within diagnoses and prescribed courses of remediation the role of emotions, thoughts, beliefs, and stress levels on physical conditions. When the yogic sages asked that essential question about where we have more power—over the internal or external—they saw it was the internal and devised yogic and meditative practices. Likewise, within the traditional Chinese culture, the Taoists also saw the value of subtle energy; at times, it seemed to be all that they valued. This led to a quite humorous misunderstanding about the cultural differences between a Chinese and an American, who has been brought up to believe in what could be tangibly seen, felt, and heard. Chi gong, the ancient science of the movement of energy, is the grandmother to tai chi and all martial arts, devised by the Taoists upon studying nature and subtle energies. You can turn to my first book, *What If There's Nothing Wrong?* written in the last of my ten years living in Asia, for an in-depth discussion of this.

Additionally, there is a vast undercurrent to both societies—Hindu Indian and Chinese—of what the food they eat does to their systems. This means that when people get a sore throat in the Chinese culture in Taiwan, they turn to a certain grass jelly drink, *xian cao*, also known on the mainland as *Gui ling gao,* served frequently as a jelly, similar to Jell-o and a dessert. Within the Indian culture, *shilajit*, a pumice scraped off high-altitude rocks, is turned to when someone needs to detox, as well as used as a daily supplement to build longevity. (I call it nasty-tasting, and I'm used to the taste of dirt, earth, weeds, and greens, as a vegetarian of twenty-three years, before the now-trendy attempts at tasty vegetarian fare had come out. My dad and brothers used to tease me, saying I was eating my jungle food. To be clear, shilajit tastes like what you would imagine it would. And I take it daily.)

These examples of food are slightly up the scale from subtle to physical energies, closer to physical energies than to subtle energies. But food breaks down, or metabolizes, returning to subtle energies. And either this subtle energy is high in life-force contents and therefore supplies a person's system with this life force, or it does not. And then there are the medicinal benefits of that food — food is thy medicine — that are also subtle energies. An awareness of the conversion role that metabolism plays, transmuting food's physical energy into subtle energies, assists us in choosing foods that will support creating more life force. And when we get to the topics of super-herbs and superfoods, we can talk specifically about what types of vital life force energy these foods are focused on creating — physical vitality, heart and spirit calming, or supporting our foundational energies.

The physical foods our eyes see, our noses smell, our tongues and throats taste, break down into subtle energies. And this metabolizing of the food — in this example let's leave out the contents of the food and focus on the person consuming the food — depends greatly on the system of the person eating it. For instance, if you notice your subtle energies not feeling up to par in vitality, and you notice this before it really physically manifests as a full-blown physical condition (as we typically do in the States), you can choose foods, beverages, spices, and other practices non-food related that can help restore your subtle energies — or here I would say vital energies — to optimal levels.

Moving on to more subtle energies now, our thoughts, feelings, and emotions all create or alchemize one form of neutral subtle energy into new energies or consciousness. At a more physical level, this translates into different biochemical messaging that occurs within our blood and system overall — not limited to only affecting the hormones—so that our bodies end up with certain tones, due to these chemical messages existing within, at a more physical level of subtle energies.

The emotions that cause certain biochemical releases either can be expressed and dissipated, or buried and stored. Typically, the energies surrounding a trauma or a dramatic event grab people's attention enough to have an impact that they don't move beyond subconsciously, and then gets buried in the subconscious and unconscious. What can occur as a result is an influence from this locked-down energy hitting the relevant chakra, and the area of the body and domain of life this relevant chakra is associated with can shut down (more on this later). Suffice it to say that strong emotional reactions and traumatic events frequently lock down energy into a block of energy, unconsciously stored in the body and within the subconscious. Since neither of those levels is conscious, we're not consciously aware of this. But these are the roots to the patterns in life of those issues that show up over and over again. And it is possible to be so unconscious of our subtle energies and so enthralled within the physical plane of life that we may not even notice these repeated patterns that lead to our suffering.

Another glimpse into subtle energies at work in our lives is when we're growing up and our neurological wiring is being formed from in the womb to around age eight. In fact, from birth to two years old, we are not even able to separate from our parents' thoughts and feelings, so we feel and think what they do. We begin to say, *no!* at that terrible-twos stage as our ego-identity begins to form, and we increasingly separate from our parents.

When we are in the process of separating from our parents, we're busy asking such questions as, "So how do I get that feeling I like so much (love) from Mom?" and, "So how does Mike, my older brother, do it here on planet Earth? Oh! He does whatever Mom and Dad want and that seems to get him that feeling I like. Okay."

And then, "Hmm, so when does Dad give me that feeling I like so much (love and approval)? Oh! He seems to like it when I'm quiet and smile a lot," and thus we conclude that being a good little girl or good little boy without much to say—especially when different from what the parents are saying—is the way to get this love and approval.

Many of us grow up feeling like we received the love and approval children naturally seek from parents and we've realized that we get this even when we don't really speak up and express ourselves. As a result, wired into our system and relevant chakras (typically here the fifth and second) will be hidden conclusions, or subconscious beliefs and unconscious conclusions. These beliefs and conclusions are behind the ensuing unconscious behavior around being quieter, inexpressive, good children abiding by the rules. We learned at this formative time that this behavior gets us love and approval in general.

You see this, don't you?

Yes?

This creates a client who comes to me wanting to feel better in her marriage and have more energy, and more presence, and more active engagement within her life. This can typically look like someone just getting by day to day, not really liking her job, coming home so tired that she then just sits at the dinner table after making dinner with her husband and child, without much real dialogue except how the day went and its events. Then dishes are done, and nighttime activities of checkout behavior ensue, due to the lack of engagement in her life and lack of excitement over her life. This can show up as watching TV or Netflix until it's time to go to bed. Her dreams wouldn't typically translate over into her daily life, because the veil between her waking life and her dream life is too thick to have this more subtle level of consciousness penetrate into her everyday operating, linear mind. This dull, lethargic mind, with a thick energy over it veiling the access to the more alive, vital life force energy that is more subtle, has a term within meditation to describe it: *laya*.

This term, laya, is used to describe a certain dullness to the mind — and therefore access to the body's subtle life force energy. It feels like a coating, serving to suppress one in coming out of this seemingly everyday life's stupor.

Kenchen Thrangu Rinpoche states: "In stupor the mind is cloudy and dull. In its obvious form, there is a loss of clarity of mind. In its subtle form there is some clarity, but it is very weak."

The prescribed antidote within Buddhist practice to this cloudy and dull tone to the mind is Awareness, or *samprajana* in Sanskrit. This awareness is cultivated from Observing our minds and gaining the awareness that we are feeling this dull cloud and lethargy to our minds. But this is based on a very pivotal premise: that we even know something else is possible.

By the time my clients get to me, they do know that something else is possible, but they don't know how to get there. Sometimes they don't even know how to articulate why they're coming to me, just that they know something is off where instead something should be more on, so to speak. They are reaching out for support to get beyond this familiar yet temporary state of mind and being. And I go to work within the chakras as well as using my intuitive holistic life coaching, where I guide clients to be increasingly mindful.

The chakras reveal to me where the block is within their unconscious beliefs, and where they're operating with unconsciousness, so we can bring awareness, or samprajana, to the current condition of a dull, lethargic mind, and being and life. This awareness and cultivated mindfulness combine together to transform our lives and lead to a gradual unwinding of the entangled unconsciousness within whatever chakras are involved.

The end result is that they are cumulatively, increasingly able to have more freed-up consciousness flowing throughout their once dull, lethargic system, so that the dullness and lethargy are replaced with brightness, sparkle, and vitality. The transformation we go through as we awaken more of our unconsciousness is a brilliant, precious process to witness, and also a deep honor to facilitate. Quite simply, it feels like I'm helping someone wake up, but from a different type of a sleep than what we think of when we go to bed at night.

One of the key areas I have focused on over the past two-and-a-half years—especially with my Tuesday night weekly group for Vibrational UPgrade clearings and activations—is addressing the subconscious blocks we have unconsciously. These blocks are sub-, or below-conscious awareness, toward allowing us to have what we desire. That sounds so simple, but it is mostly overlooked. Yet we are addressing what is typically overlooked—the subtle energies. Perhaps that's why the word *subtle* was even chosen: to describe the concept of energies that fall below the average threshold that our physically geared, physical five senses notice, categorize, identify, and label.

When asked, "If you could have anything, what would you choose? If there were no limitations, what would you go for? What would you allow yourself to desire?"

Ninety-nine percent of people asked answer with silence. They simply don't know how to answer that question. Seriously, I've watched hundreds and hundreds of people ponder that question, and it seems to send them into an unknown place, where they don't have the navigational tools to know how to proceed. This is related to my first book, *What If There's Nothing Wrong?*

When signing copies of my book, I usually wrote, "So (insert person's name), if our minds weren't busy finding something wrong, what would we then create? What else is possible?"

I found that most people had a lot of hidden conclusions around not being able to actually have what they dreamed of and desired. Much of this seems to be due to the fact that these dreams and desires are frequently hidden away—and have been for a long time—and not easily spoken about. These dreams and desires are the ones from childhood that most adults leave behind, labeling childhood dreams as "silly," "childlike," and "impractical."

As we move into this new era, this work that I do to free people—and ultimately humanity—from perceived limitations results in a clearing of the hidden conclusions that block us from even allowing ourselves to dream. These clearings also clear all the entangled blocks in our lives that show up as hesitancies toward believing that we can actually have a life built around these dreams some think of as childlike. The discouragement of what makes one inherently jubilant, and the support for the more grownup and practical choices—the kind that adults make—is rampant and mostly left unquestioned. This is part of the seriousness that perpetuates and then leaks out in subversive—and frequently destructive—ways.

Particularly in my Tuesday night clearings and activations calls, but within all my work with clients, students, and various audiences, I first raise the conscious awareness in and around the areas where they have typically been unconscious and unaware, but where they're actually making choices. For example, many function with the belief that they only have a certain level of employment and standard of living available. Yet, the actual amount of money we require is more of a choice, not a necessity. Feeling aghast and shocked are frequent reactions.

The amount of money required to have our basic needs met varies with one's values, right?

An example of this is the increasing migration, and the businesses set up around this migration, to live internationally and out of the United States. Many folks, not just retirees, are seeking an improved quality of life with a lower cost of living.

Really look at the assumptions that function below the conscious mind's consideration: if someone is in debt, the choice could be not to pay it off, right?

This is not the case for the majority of us who want to be good citizens with decent credit scores. But if a good credit score isn't valued, this lessens the pressure to create enough income to reduce the debt.

For example, a common way business owners get out from too much debt is to file bankruptcy. And even though I wasn't living in the States during the housing market collapse of 2008, I know that people walked away from their homes, unable to pay their mortgages. As a result, levels of shock rippled throughout society because *people simply didn't do that!* Now, I've returned to a housing market in which people don't stay in their homes but buy them to sell them, creating a whole new market. The popularity of house flipping has resulted in television shows based on this new trend, created from the shocking behavior of homeowners walking away from their debts and homes.

But really, wasn't it a choice by the homeowners to live beyond their means or to live at the level of pacing that was required by them to fund these new home mortgages?

If we look at it more closely, without looking for a source of blame—and by no means saying what the lending and banking industries did was right—isn't it a choice to make money a necessity?

For instance, couldn't we also choose to retire outside the United States in a country with a much lower standard of living, with a slower-paced quality of life congruent with one's desired pace of life?

Or even live in a multi-generational home with grandparents, parents, and the third generation all in one home, not because of poverty but because of the functionality of such an arrangement?

This last example can be seen in the majority of non-American, post-modern, globalized cultures that retain their cultural values rather than becoming fully westernized as they modernize.

Assumptions and hidden conclusions are implied and made when one is "keeping up with the Joneses." And those are the more obvious conclusions and assumptions, which people choose not to speak about outwardly.

But what about the more subtle—even, some would say, insidious—assumptions and conclusions, as can be seen in the amount of technical gadgets owned by the average person?

What about the assumption about consumers by the producers of the tablets and pads that we want and will purchase a lighter laptop?

And what of the choice to buy that?

Or the idea that we need to buy the latest version of the iPhone to keep up with whatever conclusions run that choice?

Often people work so unconsciously—in that unexamined need to fit in—that it feels like pressure when one sees many engaging in these behaviors. Living in a capitalistic economy, we must do it, too, or risk being an outcast. All this is silent and ripe with unconscious conclusions. Some of the more self-aware folks acknowledge that these examples are a choice. But for the majority, it is not just awareness. There are many nuanced, hidden conclusions about how people choose to spend their money. This is just one area.

It also interests me when I hear people complain about being miserable in life or wanting a different job, and when shown others who have changed these exact circumstances, they choose to conclude that they can't afford that. But when looking at their style of dress, car, and gadgets carried, it is clear where their values lie. This still reflects societal contributions to the conditioning, in that the value of feeling good isn't as important as some other aspects of life that are emphasized and physically tangible.

And in saying that, I've just created a duality that isn't real, yet seems to exist in the average American's mind. It's either focus on the surface of life—being productive and making the money to support a certain lifestyle that indicates to others and ourselves a level of success—or don't, and be someone who is more tuned inward because you'd have no money to distract or take the focus away from the simpler aspects of life. This is an oversimplification, yes. But dualistic thinking—and all its hidden assumptions—is just this. Typically, it's not even logical conclusions that affect us at the unconscious and subconscious levels.

This is changing, indeed. But what I am attempting to illustrate is how self-care and the ability to actually change the seeming set point of our daily tones and moods and thoughts—and therefore overall lives—can be possible. Folks typically don't think this. It seems like their personalities are just that—everyone knows them this way, and it's unchanging. This does vary, depending of course on the environment I'm working in and how self-aware the audience is. But typically, within the mass consciousness, it is still considered that this is something they cannot do. If Mary Ann is depressed and tends to be cynical toward life, then that is just the way she is. If Jason has a bad temper and is hostile, then that's just the way he is. Perhaps medication is considered. But that still doesn't reflect a belief that this can be fundamentally changed by addressing the foundational energy patterns and the subconscious and unconscious beliefs behind these patterns that show up and are labeled as someone's *personality*.

When presented with the opportunity to pay for something that has been shown to actually work and would help them feel more the way they want to feel, the hidden conclusions behind the level of likelihood and possibility are present within their saying no. As I have observed people in this position, it appears their Nos are almost automatic, reflecting their unconscious unawareness of this even being possible—to have a different personality.

People spend their time and money on what they value. And if we want to know what we're really valuing, we can look at our behavior. So we could even say we want a better job, but when one is put right in front of us, we could say no, doubting everything associated with this betterment. Frequently, where we are not making choices is an unconscious leaning toward the status quo, so that things remain the same. This typically results from fear, which has another entanglement of a range of subconscious beliefs that function as the blocks to saying and living more from Yes!

For example, over this past year and a half, I have noticed the surprisingly intricate series of subconscious and unconscious blocks my clients, students, and listeners and callers on my Tuesday night group Vibrational UPgrade have at both the personally conditioned level and the societal level. These blocks are about not being able to have what it is they actually dream of for their lives, and many not even able to dream of anything that they actually desire. The Tuesday night call is a bit different, as it seems to attract rather advanced, awakened people who are already looking for more.

This is beyond—but frequently includes—material items; whatever it takes for their dreams to become clear, and then actualized physically. Sometimes I'm working with folks with their biggest dream, which they're barely able to consciously admit they actually want. It's those yearnings that for most pull at the back of the mind, but remain ignored because these stirrings can't really, possibly be listened to.

Why?

Because it would disrupt their whole lives, as it seems it is perceived.

This includes the pervasive, "I'll lose people in my life if I change and go for this."

Typically this also isn't based in truth, just another automated, reactive, fear-based subconscious block. Accompanying this line of unconscious and subconscious blocks are the beliefs that the changes required for this dream to become realized would include a whole lot of upset within the family and household, and they don't want to deal with the flack their spouse, parents, children, and best friends might have about what it is they're dreaming and envisioning. So they keep it tucked in the back of their minds.

After the survival level, where basic needs are covered, luxury and comfort become the next goals. And they may obtain that luxury and comfort, but the possibility of actually being able to live their lives doing what turns them *on*, really *on*, while retaining that level of luxury does not occur to the average person. It doesn't occur to even the above-average person, who is more self-actualized, having moved beyond the survival-only focus. It's as if happiness and making a substantial income are mutually exclusive. This is becoming increasingly an outdated, subconscious belief, but it runs deep nonetheless.

One of the pieces of subconscious programming that I've seen a lot of is the idea that material success is separate from spiritual and personal fulfillment. In enter my corporate clients, who speak of having to play the game in order to live at the standard of living they're at. Meanwhile they look at me morosely, as if there's no way they can honor their fifth chakra by speaking to what they see, rather than remaining quiet and saying what's expected of them within the context they're working, a.k.a. playing the game.

One client in particular I'm thinking of was a brilliant software analyst and desperately wanted to escape from corporate America because she really enjoyed creating crafts with her mom. They even sometimes sold their crafts at local fairs. But she saw absolutely no way to be able to maintain the style of living—frequent travel, sailing, adventure sports in other countries and states than her own—if she were to depend on making a living by selling her crafts. We worked on relieving her foundational energy patterns around the entanglement of beliefs she'd mostly inherited from her dad—that work is a serious thing that burdens someone. We did this unwinding of these entangled beliefs at a subtle level, because she was already quite liberated from much of the societal conditioning. We were working on the subtlest of inherited, familial-conditioned beliefs. She wanted to stop being in pain around how she had to be in order to earn the money that afforded her the lifestyle she desired, but hadn't seen how to do this with ease. We went to work on her fifth chakra—she had chronic tight shoulders and a thyroid issue—to help her feel less restricted and limited in her choices available.

I have had many, many clients like this. Their conditioning is sometimes so strong that it's as though I am working with a certain part of them, while they look to me from another part of them, desperate for my assistance and my ability to help them go for what they really want in their lives. It's as if I'm helping them say a stronger "Yes" for the part of them that knows more is possible. At the same time I'm assisting them in successfully shutting up, or at the very least strongly quieting, that part of them so full of objections to why this dream is not possible, and their choices are limited. Lately I've come to see that what I am doing is helping people say a stronger Yes to themselves and their bigger dreams for themselves and their lives, and their freedom to live a robustly awakened life, even while that blocked part of them is still in the land of No, or contraction.

I've also observed a type of quiet desperation in which the average person is living. And so the games of checking out begin. *But* there have increasingly been good signs that the material and the spiritual, the economic activity, and the awakened heart are aligning. More and more people are dropping out of the rat race—a hamster race, with the hamster running on the wheel, round and round, getting nowhere (I'm not quite clear on the word choice, "rat"; did they in fact mean "hamster race"?)—and allowing themselves to make different choices. The latest trend in tiny houses is one example of this.

When I hosted my radio show, *Create Your Best Life Ever!* for more than two years on VoiceAmerica, I allowed one full episode with guests whom I knew locally—this was not typical for what I did on my show—to portray how the dreams of everyday folks were coming alive and becoming physically actualized businesses that made money. One of the three guests on that show was Mary Ann. It's quite a magical story, one that helps illuminate more of the subtleties around the hidden, assumed beliefs that most folks have that serve to keep them locked down in their lives, rather than growing and expanding their lives—as we are here to do.

One day in the first year of living back in the States after my decade in Asia, in the infant stages of growing what had been my part-time practice for the previous thirteen years into a full-time business, I was driving back from a meeting. I had met with some folks who owned a local business that worked with retraining the brains of kids who had difficulty concentrating and focusing, using a somewhat holistic approach.

As I was driving away from that meeting, I suddenly heard a command, "Turn there!" and so I immediately turned my steering wheel to the left and pulled into one of Florida's many strip malls.

Once in the parking lot, I wondered where I was going. There were about ten businesses in this little strip.

I saw a chiropractor's office and pulled in there. I walked in the front door without question as to what I was doing, and began to speak with the woman who was working behind the desk. She was easy to talk to, and I found myself engaging in a longer conversation upon first meeting her than I'd expected. Still freshly back from living among the Chinese, where no extra information is typically given in initial conversations and a more reserved approach is favored, I found this surprising. Instead of the rather tight holding back in a reserved yet light way, which I had become more accustomed to living with in Asia, I was easily pouring forth conversation, without self-monitoring the way I'd learned to living as an expat among the Chinese. I liked this! It reminded me more that I was home, in a sense. The Chinese way I'd become accustomed to was certainly different from the more extroverted American style, especially the friendliness in the likes of the average person in the sunshine state. In fact, before moving to Asia, I had been always told I was extremely extroverted, considered almost instantly by most I met to be considered the lively one.

Those ten years of living as an ex-pat among the Chinese, while also learning increasingly the practices of the subtle energies, had changed that extroversion to a more balanced flow. Plus, at that first meeting with Mary Ann, I was still enmeshed within the cultural differences, which appeared to be much harsher upon return to one's home country and re-integrating than when facing the exoticism of the host culture in the foreign country. It had been confusing at times, to say the least; that is, if I were looking for solid labels for whom I'd become. Part of this for me was even more of that great teacher of the mandate for fluidity.

Back to that first meeting with Mary Ann. I told her my background briefly and asked if we could set up an appointment with the chiropractor; maybe there was something I could offer him and his practice. I was talking from a place of both curiosity and a question, because I had no clarity around the specifics of what I was doing, nor why I was doing it.

She booked an appointment for the following Monday, my only non-client, non-teaching, non-group-healing office day reserved for outreach. So I returned the following Monday and spoke with the chiropractor, and we agreed to begin to work together to see what would emerge, with us each presenting what our unique tools were. The second or third time I met with him, I realized that I wasn't there to work with him as much as with the woman behind the desk—Mary Ann.

I said to her on my way out of his office that day, "I don't think I'm meant to be working with him. I think I pulled in here that day because I am meant to be working with you. Why is that?"

She looked at me and said, "Well, I've been feeling pretty stuck in my life and have been asking recently, 'Okay, what's next? What is it that I'm meant to be doing?' Because this job isn't it."

She looked at me with such a dead-on glare that if I hadn't a sense of humor, or hadn't learned to take things personally, I would've thought she'd wanted to strangle me!

Smiling at the look on her face, I laughed and said, "Okay, Mary Ann, why don't you come in and see me and we'll do a session for *you*?"

She appeared to understand my laugh and seemed encouraged that I had in fact chosen this behavior. I looked at my calendar and saw the next available appointment. She then looked at hers and saw this was fine, and so she was booked.

Mary Ann and I began to work together. Apparently, she'd spent the previous thirteen years on antidepressants. She was married and had two grown daughters. Mary Ann was fifty-six years old at that time. We were starting to get to what I'll call *the medium level* of her unconscious and subconscious beliefs that acted as blocks in her life. We'd already made much progress clearing out the topmost layers that had revealed themselves as ready to be transformed. We were just getting to the beginnings of what beliefs had created the foundational energy patterns that had kept her choices and her life locked in and seemingly limited to her.

My birthday fell around this time. It was my second birthday after my return to the States. Mary Ann made the first homemade birthday cake I had since being back. It was some kind of lava cake, and it was outrageously good. She had asked me what flavors I preferred about a month before, but I had no idea what she was up to. I'd responded that dark chocolate and raspberry are one flavor combination I tend to dig. On the day of my birthday, she brought it right to my front door, on a tray and all, with candles and a smile. The thoughtfulness and graciousness were enough for me. But, oh my God, I was so ecstatic to also bite into that moist, warm, chocolate deliciousness! I am not a cake eater (brownies and chocolate chip cookies — okay!). So I expected to simply tolerate the actual eating of the cake with gratitude, finishing only half a piece, as I do. Not this time! So much so that this has now become my birthday ritual — Mary Ann applying her baking talents for my birthday.

What surprised me was that I had not known she was also a baker—and a good one. I had known she had repair abilities as my seamstress, and some creative abilities, too, with table runners she made from textiles. But what I had not understood was that Mary Ann had her bachelor's degree in home economics. Further, upon graduation she had opened up her own cake shop and bakery. In addition to this, the table runners she worked with had actually been a part-time gig for a span of years.

At the point I was learning this, er, somewhat key information, she was selling her creations at all the local artisans' craft markets that are so prolific here in Florida, especially in the non-summer months.

I had met Mary Ann when she was an administrative assistant, and she told me it was the umpteenth administrative job she'd had throughout her professional life. (She has a video on my testimonials page—in that video she actually names the number of jobs.) What I had known about her was that she sewed, and the table textiles that she'd sold at various local arts and crafts festivals didn't provide a good return on her investment in time, energy, and money, so she'd stopped. She had become disheartened from doing these craft fairs because basically, those table runners—in contrast to what she's doing now—had been boring and stale and stagnant for her to create. They were below her capabilities, barely activating her abundant creativity.

During our course of unwinding those core energetic patterns, as some of the unconsciousness within her fifth chakra began to rise to the surface, it became clear to me that she expected to be burdened with living a life of duty. Now, this lovely woman hailed from the northeast United States, where the Puritans had quite an influence, in the cold, dismally weathered state of

Maine, comparative to the sunshine state. I should know — I was born and raised there myself, in suburbia south of Boston. But what also came out of progressively clearing her throat center and loosening up the noose of restrictions on her and her life (the fifth chakra — the one of creativity and choices and courage, which will be progressively revealed later) is that she was highly spiritual, but had become shut down to organized religion. One of her two daughters had in fact become a missionary, which befuddled Mary Ann, causing her to distance herself a bit from this daughter.

During the course of unwinding the foundational energy patterns in the relevant chakras where they were bound up, it came up that she'd had some sort of past within organized religion. She was not even aware, really, nor would she have readily admitted at that time, that she was spiritual. Mary Ann had closed down to this part of herself, due to her seemingly inexplicable distaste for organized religion. There were no big dramas to point to in her childhood to explain such a strong push away from organized religion, so I was guided to go in further to this lockup within her consciousness.

When I did, she was standing so I could muscle test her system to assess what subconscious beliefs and the related family around these beliefs were that acted as blocks within her. We were using her body to tell us what her subconscious believed, or what unconscious beliefs her mind-body-spirit system actually held locked in place within her consciousness and therefore body, prior to doing the clearings. She remained standing while I did a few clearings on the initial blocks she'd tested positive for.

When I tested for the belief, *You are meant to be burdened*, what popped into my consciousness immediately was a vision of piercing clarity of Mary Ann dressed as some kind of nun.

She was in a dark monastery built of stone that remained cold year round, and she seemed to be in charge of the operations of the monastery and nuns. Next what was given to me was seeing and sensing Mary Ann as resentful of all the burden and restriction, making many sacrifices within her own life in order to do this. I saw with my inner eye and sensed with my intuitive sensory equipment that in that lifetime, Mary Ann had been miserable and unfulfilled. And it was in the Northeast, it seemed, or in the United Kingdom, perhaps even Ireland, where Mary Ann had some genetic links. I couldn't tell and for me that detail was superfluous, and more of the story about that life was unimportant. What was and is always central for me with my work is that I assist my clients in getting free. I refer my clients to others who have that desire to uncover the stories. I just want more freedom for us all, not more information. So I'll bring forth the most pertinent information, just to assist in clearing out restrictive blocks. A few times I've had clients ask for more and I've given it. But when I've done so, the nature of the session was more about play than it was about clearing.

So once I cleared, *You are meant to be burdened,* Mary Ann fell to her knees onto the floor of the healing studio room we were in.

This is the one and only time I've seen such a physically dramatic response to the clearings I do. The outcomes of the clearings can be dramatic, yes. But not the initial reaction. Typically, it's shivers, yawns, and legs and arms flicking and kicking as the energy gets through to the block that is being destroyed; but now energy is able to get through as it clears, causing a muscular twitch. Just as frequently, folks do what I call *knock out*: they go into sleep and return within typically a few minutes.

Many folks frequently go to sleep with my clearings, which is a gracious act on behalf of the conscious mind, stepping out of the way, so to speak, and allowing the higher vibrations to go to work that the conscious mind is yet consciously able to field. This allows these higher, healing vibrations to go in and cause the upgrade in the beliefs, clearing out the old block and its density. It's really cool to watch people remain relatively alert and awake during the first twenty minutes of the hour of clearings on my clearings and activations call, and once I hit a core or at least a deep block of theirs, their heads fall back and they just get knocked out. It is one of the more — of the many — fascinating aspects to this work that I do.

But I'd not had anyone lose their ability to stand and fall to the floor! It was ironic and no mistake that what was being cleared was her belief, likely reinforced through many repeated lifetimes of this type of configuration in her life, of being burdened. And she fell to the floor in order to become unburdened. What was also cool was that this proceeded to wipe out, as we would see later, her hesitation with organized religion. What she started to create after the very next session were no longer table runners, no. Instead, they were brilliantly colored fabrics and textiles she ordered from around the world, inlaid with sacred symbols from all the world's spiritual traditions. But I'm getting ahead of myself just a bit here.

We slowly got her onto the table, and I continued to do one or two more clearings to help her subconscious and unconscious blocks toward religion and spirituality. These subconscious beliefs had been functioning as blocks toward Mary Ann stepping into the life she desired and were some of the deeper, buried, entangled beliefs. We were only able to get to unwinding, clearing, and sorting out these beliefs once we'd already cleared out some more surface-level subconscious blocks that created an unconsciousness for Mary Ann about what choices were even available to her.

She was fifty-six when we began working together. Her two grown daughters both graduated with their bachelor's degrees, and both had degrees in different art mediums. Mary Ann's husband of nearly forty years had been working at a stable governmental job for quite some time. Mary Ann was lowering her dosage of anti-depressants with her doctor when we first began working together, so that ultimately I was working with a brain that had been on them for more than a decade. Within her married life, Mary Ann had dutifully left aside herself and raised her girls, getting administrative jobs where she felt drawn to work, and sometimes just where she could get the work.

But she had that bachelor's degree in home economics. When I asked her why she chose that degree, she said back then it was the only acceptable way to make money for a married woman and mother who was creative. Since age four she had dreamed, literally and figuratively, of becoming an artist. But she put that on the back burner in order to do what was the acceptable thing at the time for creative artists who were also a married with two kids to raise: she got a job teaching home economics. Eventually, after her daughters left the house and went off for their art degrees, Mary Ann had brought back the arts with the textiles she created as those table runners.

Once we cleared the blocks around burden and organized religion, Mary Ann increasingly gained energy and vitality. What also seemed to basically explode—once unleashed—was her creativity! That continues to this day, as she goes about creating her Awakened Fibers, the name she has given her sacred textiles business. It has taken off. At first, Mary Ann and I decided to attend local outdoor holistic mind-body-spirit events together, under one tent. I was already going to them, and as Mary Ann continued to have these ideas for new textiles embodying sacred energy that she was getting in touch with within herself, she had products to sell, so we chose to have some fun under one tent.

In many of the ensuing sessions after that major breakthrough about being unburdened, I introduced to Mary Ann sacred symbols from the yogic world, the Buddhist world, the Taoist culture, the Mayans, and other sacred symbols from other cultures. She would bring over new fabrics she'd imported from Bali, and I'd see symbols in them—not really there—and I'd go get a book or my laptop and show her the symbol, and then *bam*! I said no more, and her mad creative genius took it and ran with it. She was on fire.

When we began working together, Mary Ann came across as cynical, with barely enough energy to get through her stupid, boring days doing what boring, stupid stuff she was doing with her little life. You could ask her. It's comical, the contrast now. That negativity has transmuted into this fierce, potent desire and commitment to herself, her craft, and her creative genius, blessing her life and the many others who buy her sacred textiles.

It was funny, watching folks magnetically pulled from across a field that was a part of the venue for various outdoor expos, zooming right up to one of Mary Ann's racks and proceeding to look through her textiles, exclaiming as they found the one, two, or three sacred symbols they were looking for. People have hung them up in their meditation rooms, above their altars, in their centers—as I have my brilliant chakra banner she created just for me—while many also gift Mary Ann's Awakened Fibers to loved ones they want to assist and reassure in their awakening process. And frequently, it's not even that conscious, people are attracted to whatever sacred images Mary Ann places on brilliant, exotic fabrics that her eyes see to blend. It's brilliant work, and it's been such full-on fun watching her work inspire so many others! As her business continued to boom, and her creativity consistently unleashed itself, she needed a full tent to accommodate all the fabrics she was creating in her sewing room or laboratory. We no longer share a tent at outdoor expos.

Many months later, when musing over that day when I was so magnetized right to the door of the office where she was working, and all that had transpired since, I said to her, "So all that we've been able to shift within you and transform, and looking at you now, this all helps me understand why my antennae pulled me so strongly right to you. My personal GPS was not messing around. It got me right there into that strip mall (she was no longer working there) and to the office door you were on the other side of."

As she explained to me, "A couple weeks before that day you first came in, I had asked the universe why I had to live under a dark cloud all the time. I had even reached out to one of our patients, who was some kind of intuitive and psychic, to tell her about the dark cloud and she said 'Well, you created it!' which did not help me at all. I did not have any concept of what that meant, so all I felt was blame and shame. Then you showed up."

For increasing the speed and ease of her transformation, and to get her freer in an increased, fuller way, I suggested that Mary Ann also receive training in meditation and mindfulness, so she attended my weekly Vibrational UPgrade meditation and yoga class. In this class I teach what was known to be Buddha's most frequently taught meditation technique, of all the various ones he taught. This particular meditation technique returns our consciousness to our bodies, and cultivates an awakened and fully embodied Presence. This is also key in disengaging from the checkout habits folks have when they don't like their lives, and instead choose to space out of their embodied existence, and seemingly hover above their bodies. The accompanying choice, albeit unconscious, is to then check out with various behaviors—whether that be watching a lot of TV, shopping, drinking, eating, Internet porn, continuously with others, continuously racing around without any time to be still—whatever the disconnect habitual tendencies are.

For Mary Ann, with this practice established in meditation for her, the mindfulness cultivated as a result reinforced for her at the daily level the disconnect we'd created in her foundational energy patterns. She could take any reappearance of those once-cynical, negative thoughts—focused on all the various ways limitations showed up in and around her—without that attached seriousness she once had. Adding to that the yoga asanas (postures) and toning we did for the chakras, we were able to keep the momentum building around the newer, fresher energies of expansion, choice, creativity, and courage to consistently choose this for herself, rather than giving in to the old, stale voices of the ego-mind, with its focus on the status quo, limitation, and thus stagnancy.

By working on and cultivating the Observer in her, she could see and learn how her mind throws out the repetitive thoughts it does, but she was now not at the mercy of them. She'd learned not to believe her thoughts. I remember her reporting to me about when she was in the dentist's chair, she heard my voice from class, reminding her to let go of the thought and return to the breath, which seemed to help her with her mental noise around the dental procedure. Good stuff! It's not just applicable to coming out from the self-suppression of listening to the old, limiting beliefs that the ego-mind offers up in order to maintain the status quo.

You see?

What she was also able to create was freedom from identifying herself as her mind, thoughts, and beliefs. I've seen this in all my clients who are students in my Vibrational UPgrade meditation and yoga class, as well as folks who are my students only in this class. Indeed, it's been an activation of her Higher Self, as she increasingly learned to let go of her Lower Self or ego-mind-based identity she'd known herself to be since she could remember. And it has been therefore easier for her to access continuing energy that builds her creativity, vitality, and expansion.

This is key: Once people detach from the old negative voices in their heads that serve to keep them limited in the comfort zone of the status quo, and thus increasingly let go of any of the old triggers, this allows for a moving beyond their previous level of living. This is one of the primary geniuses that I love about the Vibrational UPgrade work I do. The foundational energy patterns getting cleared disconnect folks from their blocks. This disconnects even more the charge that the blocks—beliefs—used to keep in place with their ensuing old triggers.

Those triggered reactions show up as seemingly automatic behavior when in that environment or around those people, as if there is no choice involved, right?

There is always choice.

But it appears to the conscious, non-Observing person of the subtle energies that these blocks and unconscious beliefs keep folks locked into their old patterns, and simply show up as well: "That's just the way it is."

So mindfulness and detachment make it much easier. To gain these tools is to gain freedom from your old self. To gain freedom from your old self means moving beyond your previous limitations.

To do this means the low energy and low vitality and maybe depression lift and are replaced by vibrant, vital life force. This is because we are meant to expand, consistently, ongoing—it is the nature of all life. Therefore, one can notice how our systems release more chi, or vital life force energy, whenever growth and expansion are being called for. If we aren't tuned into these subtle energies, then we'll miss the cues of shutdown in our emotional, mental, and energetic lives. These cues show up frequently as lethargy, that gray cloud, not feeling like oneself, low energy, low sex drive, not much creativity, and a low-level hum in the background overall, pulling one's energy, life, and living down. Stress responses result from this, as it is easier from this lower threshold of awakened vital life force energy when on this track to have the mind view environmental cues as stressors. And the body then reacts with the hormonal cascades in response to this interpretation of something stressful. If we were at a higher hum of living as the backdrop for our energy, the tendency to be reactive and interpret environmental situations and factors decreases, as we have more balance and energy, and feel connected to this Higher Self's inherent intuition, grace, and ease. And it's also easier to react when one has low energy or depression. It can be a cycle, yes, because each track has its own momentum. All thoughts do. So when we're shrinking back into the comfort zone our ego-mind prefers and not going for what our Higher Self is subtly pointing to, we then suppress this vital life force energy by not choosing to use it for the expansion it is there for. So we "deep-press" back down the energy—and end up depressed.

Mary Ann gradually began to allow herself to recognize that she was actually free. And I began to see a smile pervade her face, consistently.

She also—upon reviewing her story as I portrayed here—said, "You may want to mention that I have not taken or felt the need to take any antidepressants for the last three years."

The voice that she had listened to for decades within her has been replaced by her awakened, enlivened creativity—and she's blessing many because of her choice to go for more.

Chapter Four

The Effects of Blocks and Chakras

Until you make the unconscious conscious, it will direct your life and you will call it fate.

~ Carl Jung

The goal of life is to make your heartbeat match the beat of the Universe.

~ Joseph Campbell

When you are inspired by some great purpose, some extraordinary project, all your thoughts break their bonds; your mind transcends limitations, your consciousness expands in every direction, and you find yourself in a new, great, and wonderful world. Dormant forces, faculties, and talents become alive, and you discover yourself to be a greater person by far than you ever dreamed yourself to be.

~ Patanjali

When a *chakra*, or *wheel,* as it is used in Sanskrit, is unable to turn the vital life force energy within that region of the body and out to the domain of life that it's responsible for, this region of the body and domain of life suffers from not receiving vital life force energy. This gives us a sense of grayness, lethargy, no energy, no excitement, no juice for life, no creativity, lack of inspiration, dullness within our relationships, a lack of sharpness in the colors as we look out onto the world, lack of sex drive, lack of clarity, foggy thinking, disconnection from others while feeling lonely and isolated, disconnection from the natural world, nature, and the more primal essence of life—even the wildness that shows up as our courage and freedom to express ourselves. Chronic pain, dis-ease, and all these other symptoms are some of the most fundamental aspects affected when our beliefs are unconscious and subconscious and are negatively affecting a chakra so that it cannot deliver the fresh vital life force to our body and lives.

That may be enough motivation to cause someone to begin the self-discovery process. And more than that, if you go to my website and look at the *Chakra Attunement Audio Series*, you'll see a list of the various effects each chakra has on the physical, mental, emotional, and spiritual levels. This is meant to help you assess yourself and in what part of your life and body you're experiencing a lockdown on your energy so that it seems you're stuck. In a way, that's a great description to use, because it communicates a feeling for the dynamics of the energy flows: they're not flowing; they're stuck. Another effect of these subconscious programs and unconsciousness shows up as you keep repeating the same patterns that aren't leading you to well-being or thriving in that area of your life.

For example, if money and having more than enough money has always been a challenge, then it is quite likely that we first need to look at the foundational beliefs that got wired into your root chakra. We're not so much looking at the subconscious and unconscious beliefs and then processing them as we are clearing out the foundational energy patterns in the unconsciousness so we can disentangle the energy that has become a block within this chakra and area of your life. I love this aspect of my work. Talking about something over and over again takes energy that is moving all the time, and locks it down, over and over again.

This creates something more real and more solid. I used to say in my start-up marketing blurbs: "Less talk therapy, more results!"

And it's true. Staying at the talk-therapy level—my first major in college, which I left because I found it so incomplete and thus ineffective—keeps one at that very cerebral level that maintains continuing the same behaviors because it is done at a conscious level. If these blocks existed at a conscious level, well then, they wouldn't be blocks! But it's because these blocks reside in the unconscious and subconscious systems within each person that they then lead to automatic behaviors that the conscious mind simply doesn't function at a level to see. This is precisely why it is so helpful to slow down enough to be able to pick up on the triggers behind the automatic behavioral responses. Becoming more inquisitive toward our minds and thoughts is the way to begin to unravel this. But to be clear, it is not meant to be analyzed. These are foundational energy patterns; it is the energy that requires an unwinding around where the subconscious and unconscious have created the beliefs in order to affect behavioral change, ultimately.

Going back to the example of feeling like one never has enough money no matter the actual amount, this again is the root chakra, which is the foundation of the chakra column. Thus it is the chakra at the perineum and as it is described on my website for the *Chakra Attunement Audio Series*, the domain in life the root chakra covers at each level of existence are:

Physical: obesity; clumsiness; feet and leg deformities, aches and pains, general issues; spinal alignment issues; foundational immune system disorders; eating disorders related to feelings of eating in a hoarding way, like there's never enough; physical hoarding; abundance and financial issues, regardless of whether you have money or not, but feel it's never enough or you feel there isn't enough, a.k.a. *the lack paradigm*, and its ensuing beliefs and behaviors.

Mental, Spiritual, and Emotional: not having a connection with one's body, not comfortable within your body or with your body; walk into social settings, offices, groups and never feel like you belong or have the right to be there; not feeling safe and secure in your world and in our world; feeling that there's a constant threat to attend to; general fear.

And included within this MP3 product are the key traumas cleared from physical abuse and neglect of basic needs growing up.

So, as you can see, this chakra operates at the foundational level of life, as it correlates to the foundational part of our bodies and lives overall. At this foundational level, our root chakra is where we most combine energy into form. Accordingly, it also represents our primal connection, too, to the Earth's matrix to all of life, because the Earth is our foundational support: where our food is grown, our currencies are derived, and our base for building domiciles for our families and ourselves exists. This is true whether we live in a skyscraper or a one-story home or mud-and-grass-thatched hut; it is all based on its foundation in the Earth. This is how the chakra system works; the location of the chakras in the body gives meaning to the respective levels of consciousness.

And together these seven chakras describe a profound formula for wholeness and a template for transformation. You can go over the different chakras' aspects at the physical, emotional, mental, and spiritual levels.

I guarantee you will identify at least two different chakras that will be like a *bam*! in you, and you'll say, "Those are my issues!"

Everybody does it. No matter how thriving they are. Because we're looking at a system that is designed to support us to exist in bliss, or *ananda*. I have never met anyone who didn't have at least one key chakra that was the remaining area of life to tone up.

And quite frankly, this chakra column has so much to it as we go into the various types of energies that are available in the entire pool of consciousness. As the ancient yogic masters later Buddhism—particularly Tibetan Buddhism—understood and then practiced and taught, to start with clearing out the blocks to the chakras' foundational energy patterns is only the beginning. These are cultures that have studied longevity for centuries.

For example, there is the famous kundalini energy. We are not getting into this at all here; it's way too involved, nor is that the intention of this book. Here, in this book, it seems like what is being asked to be brought forward is a focus on Awakened energy for this Awakened time, in this new era of Humanity's Spiritual Awakening. Kundalini is not the same type of energy, of bubbling life force energy like *prana*; it is different, and with an entirely different level of practitioner who is ready to approach working with the kundalini energy. It is not the light kind of effervescent energy, like kombucha tea gives off. It is heavier, denser, and more complex. It moves slower and only under certain conditions does it move at all. We're looking at the constantly moving chi, or prana, or vital life force energy that animates all of life.

Returning now to the more introductory levels that are more functional for the majority, the fact that the chakras spin—when open, like wheels—comes from the intersecting of two basic currents, one from above and one from below. This tells us that both what are above and below are equally central to our well-being and thriving. Some like to say the lower chakras represent the Lower Self, and they kind of turn their noses up at working with the body and its urges and more basic functions. Instead, they turn their focus to the higher chakras, of the spirit and of more mental activity, relegating the intellect to the higher, more evolved positioning.

Yet one of the key foundational energy patterns that folks come to me with is migraines—and they're increasing. They have too much energy at the two highest chakras, due to this emphasis on mental activity, and so the energy isn't dropping down through the neck, or throat chakra, and distributing down the *sushuma*, the central column for the seven primary chakras, and getting down to the root chakra. The energy is congested up in the head, it is corked at the neck, so to speak, and not able to spread throughout one's system, along the *nadis* that the vital life force flows along, as it is directed out from an open chakra. The fifth chakra usually plays a key role here too in this pattern, as if providing the corking—or open flow—at the neck, where the energies from the head could drop down and distribute to the lower chakras.

Check this out, though: an open and balanced root chakra helps ground the vital life force more, so the more we are grounded, the less energy gets bottled up at the head. Migraines aren't the only outcome I've seen of this pattern; it can also show up as difficulty concentrating, being easily distracted, losing one's balance easily, and other typical outcomes that would make sense if you heard them. The energy is not dropping down into the body out of the head so that the vital life force energy is able to spread down the butt and thighs and hamstrings and calves and ankles and feet to the tips of the toes. The toes—all but the pinky—are also where the end points of all the major meridians in Chinese medicine, such as acupuncture, are located, and where all the chi dumps down into before circulating back up. Meridians and nadis, from the Chinese culture and the Hindu Indian yogic cultures respectively, in our context both do the same thing in that they flow the chi, or prana, or vital life force energy throughout the system, as if highways, routes, and roads, with the sushuma, or central main column for the chakras being the primary interstate.

Our subconscious and unconscious beliefs clamp down this flow if our beliefs close down a chakra. When we are full of energy, it is reasonable to assess that we have a good, balanced root chakra. Part of being responsible for the foundational part of our systems means that the root chakra is involved in the foundational support systems for life—energy and immunity. It is truly an ingenious system that has never failed me once to explain as the mind (subconscious and unconscious), spirit, and body intersect what is going on within a person. It is such a reliable, consistent road map. You could, in fact, read the testimonials on my website to glean this. So it seems that that chakra system really helps us appreciate and see how there is such an effect from our hidden beliefs throughout our minds, bodies, and spiritual systems. It is also very much why the yogis and the Taoist chi gong masters know to work with subtle energy for health, vitality, and well-being at all levels of the human system. It is so far beyond just a New-Age fluff of nonsense.

To help further illustrate this, the word *pranayama* derives from the Sanskrit words *prana* and *ayama*, translating as "life force" and "expansion" respectively. It is a common term for various techniques for accumulating, expanding, and working with prana. In yoga, pranayama usually refers to a practice based on detailed and specific breathing techniques. It is important for the advanced yoga student to master and work with prana, in order to clean out and open all the nadis, and subsequently reach higher states of spiritual development.

In the Hindu philosophy, it is believed that a person who masters the flow of prana can learn to transfer and use it to manipulate the outside world. Accordingly, one can then heal other people and perform otherwise seemingly impossible feats due to this self-mastery of the flow of prana, and therefore the ability to move energy and transform prana, or vital life force energy in general. If one has cleaned out the chakras and prana is freely and vibrantly flowing through all chakras, then it is safe to conclude that a person has a higher vibration, as the lower, congealed, and congested energy that weighs one down and serves to block the chakras has been cleared. So the density has been transmuted into more light and consciousness (many consider that one and the same) and is able to do what we're here to do: create our lives as the co-creators we are meant to be, using this life force, directed in the way that most causes our systems to thrive. This requires a level of self-actualization, to use one term; in another, a being whom is awakened to his or her own vital life force energy, with creative self-expression and creation an inherent part of this opened system, able to wield energy. More on this later, in the advanced section.

I know that I absolutely make sure to do *nadi shodhana pranayama*, the alternate nostril breathing pranayama, every day. It is also one of the primary tools that I give to my audiences, no matter the content or scope of the topic, because it always can be contextualized. And more importantly, it is such an invaluable tool that I want as many people to know it as possible. It has a long, long list of benefits. The biggest relief I've seen it give folks over and over again is decongesting their sinus cavities, as well as bringing in immediate peace and calm and an ability to focus. This is because when working with the nasal cavity we are in part working with the sixth chakra. In fact, you can view testimonials about this on my website and Facebook pages. The alternate nostril breathing pranayama also seems really beneficial in assisting folks to come out of the fight-or-flight mode, and from being overwhelmed by anxiety. It has a brilliant, penetrating, calming effect on the entire system, and takes one out of the sympathetic nervous system to the parasympathetic nervous system.

Yet in the West, and in particular the United States, we are not guided to acknowledge the importance of what goes on under the surface. So if we are angry, we're considered to have a bad temper. What typically is going on is that the anger rises up, correlated to the third chakra, because we have had our boundaries crossed. And the third chakra is where our translation of how we fit with others intertwines with how we fit with ourselves and our self-esteem and self-confidence. This is also where our empathic equipment resides, and this chakra's element is fire. This is a very complex issue, and one that I find myself frequently working on with folks who consider themselves codependent or too sensitive or who feel others' energy too much. For our purposes here, the emotions *are* in fact information, and they contain wisdom in the form of a way to see into what our systems at a spiritual level, or essence level, are feeling from within.

Contrast this with the five physical senses geared toward the data they pick up in the physical world, and there is the completeness of our systems, in its masculine and feminine balance. The masculine is the outward manifestation, the yang, the physically tangible, and the making of the subtle into the physical. The feminine is the inward, the yin, the subtle realms, where all that is physically manifested first begins. And this is the realm of subtle energy, emotions, feelings, and thoughts. The parasympathetic nervous system is the feminine, according to the yogic tradition, and it is the calming action for our bodies. The sympathetic nervous system is the masculine one, and it is the activating one, as in fight or flight.

In my ten years living in Asia, I heard many times and saw it myself that America is a masculine, or yang, country and Taiwan and India are yin, or feminine, countries. I feel that is true in just that these ancient cultures of the Chinese and Hindu Indian knew that the power resides in the internal rather than the external. And so they developed practices to help us keep these sources of such power clear and vital and attuned to the power in all of life—that vital life force energy that exists within us and runs throughout our chakra system, and that vital life force energy, or chi, or prana, that exists throughout all of nature. We are trained to connect with and cultivate this in the practice of chi gong to cultivate our own chi, or vital energy. And perhaps it's the source of prana, or vital life force, that keeps the chakras flowing in this consciousness, or chi, or prana, or vital life force energy—when allowed to be open because we've cleared out unconscious and subconscious blocks that stop up the flow of consciousness throughout the system.

Vital love force energy keeps us alive, vital, awakened, and ready to thrive, depending on the coagulation or stagnancy in the flow in response to our unconsciousness.

Egoism is the same as *the Do-er*, or the productive one. It is said within the yoga and meditation worlds that being the doer narrows one's access to the prana life force.

There is a frequently overlooked aspect that yet again today I was talking about with clients. We are not trained in the West, particularly in the States, to pay heed to these subtle energies, or our life force. We look at something once it has manifested. Here's an example: My client, a married woman in her fifties, a retired CPA and later math teacher, is taking care of her elderly parents, both of whom have dementia. When she returns home from a day of working with them, which is now her full-time job, she finds herself reaching for the pasta, bread, chips, and coffee. It's quick sugar. Her system is looking for quick forms of energy, because she is drained. However, she stops there and makes herself bad and wrong for what she thinks of as the indulgence and the weakness that led to her indulgence. That's at the physical level.

What I took her back to, retraining her Observer, was to a point when she was with her parents and she began to notice she was starting to think foggily, starting to become overwhelmed and feel as if she was getting spun up in their demented — they have dementia — worlds. She attended to them as if they were still her two parents, because that's who they have been her entire life, without a sense of what this was doing to her own system, energetically, emotionally, and spiritually.

But what she also said, which is the key indicator to her subtle energies, was, "I feel like when I get home I am just so drained. I lay down, and I feel like all the life has been sucked out of me. Like my spirit is just gone."

To which I responded, "It is. That's precisely why you feel the way you do."

"What?" she asked.

I said, "You chose to use the exact phrases you did because that particular wording is your intuition helping you interpret your body's sensations and responses and reactions to how you take care of your parents."

"But I didn't get anything visual. You get stuff that's visual."

She has also been a student of my Chakra Flow Energy Medicine up to Level II of the three levels there currently are, so I've been teaching and guiding her through her intuitive development. The woman is strongly, inherently intuitive, and is a powerhouse in her own right.

When I first met her — before she'd retired from teaching to take care of her elderly parents full time — I thought to myself: *Wow, this woman is a fireball! Cool!* And I proceeded to get to know her.

"Yes, I do," I said. "But I also get stuff that is not visual, just in words. And so the words you just said to me, 'the life drained out of me' is precisely what has happened. You're in an environment where two people are on their way out; one is closer to dying than the other. They don't have much life force left, so they're sucking off of their dutiful daughter's abundant supply. And without you knowing it, but with the cording at your power centers and your childhood triggers of being a good little girl and dutiful daughter, they're able to pull at you on those cords, or that conditioning. So you give them more than a detached caregiver would, you give them *your* energy, in a very direct way. So that is why you come home with your body — not your mind — craving the instant source of energy."

This took her a while to understand, because we're not used to going into the dynamics of energy and looking at the subtle, and paying it heed for the seeding ground and the field it is for all creation. Everything exists in the subtle energies before it becomes something physical. And her focus was on the physical act of eating food that she otherwise wouldn't — under normal conditions — eat. And then I drew her attention to the next level of the physical, closer to subtle energy, and spoke again about her bodily sensations of feeling like the life had been sucked out of her.

"It's not just your emotions that communicate wisdom. We are talking about your energy levels, which are a measure of your own life force energy. And you had the Observer engaged enough to be able to not just give in to how you felt, but to also Observe how you felt, be with it, ask questions, and receive the intuitive guidance in the form of 'I feel drained of all life force. I have no energy.' Your intuition was showing you what had happened in that exchange of energy with your parents. Everything is about energy flow, and in one situation one person can command, demand, and control the energy flow more than another and that's what we think of as power. Everything comes down to power, and that is looked at within as how the energy is flowing."

She was with me so far, so I decided to use another route to help her get this even more clearly. "Do you remember the Weebles toys?"

"Yes!"

"Okay."

She was on her tummy now, with her face in the face cradle and I was working on the energy centers on her back, so I used my foot to show her the movements, putting it under the face cradle.

"So you know how they would tilt to the left and then tilt to the right and even back and forth?" I used my foot to move in the directions I was describing, asking, "Are your eyes open?"

"Yes. I can see what you mean."

"Okay. So since you were a little girl, your mother has always hammered you with criticism, right?" And I moved my foot in toward my body, indicating her mother leaning in to her.

"Yes!"

"And so she would push in on you, right? Forcing her view of the world onto you?"

"Yes!"

"And so, okay, what you typically have done," we'd been working together for at least eight months so I knew what we were working on quite intimately, "is you wouldn't necessarily lean back into her." I moved my foot back in the opposite direction back toward where her pretend mother's corner was, or side. "Instead, you felt pushed by her and so you responded with feeling smaller and contracted back within yourself, right?" and I moved my foot back in the other direction again, toward her side.

"Yes," she was following me, but in the midst of garnering a whole new understanding so I could feel a lot was shifting within her at this point.

"So if she is used to ruling over you, getting you to contract back into yourself, and you're used to having to come over to her, in your acts of wanting to please her and gain this essential authority figure's approval and love, then the energy is contained within her and her corner, and you're coming out of your corner — or center — constantly. She has been controlling the energy flow, with you in reaction to how she pushes the energy. And so now she's so used to having your energy to push into and receive your energy back in your attempts to please her and gain her approval, that she has been dominating the power, or controlling the flow of energy. You see this, right?"

"Yes."

She was a bit more tentative now, as the unconscious patterns was being brought to light, and there was consciousness around this pattern getting created.

In the same steady, paced way, I continued, "So now, with you being that dutiful daughter she so expects, she's used to getting what she wants from you. And now it's life force. So you could either pull back now." I moved my foot back into her corner and said, "And if you did, what would that cause her to do?"

She hesitated a moment and said, "I guess she'd lean over toward me, right?"

Now it was my turn. "Yes."

After a pause, while I proceeded down to her lower power centers on her back, removing my foot from underneath the face cradle, I then said, "So she's now looking for you, with you pulled back. And if you want to have some credit and gratitude given to you, then you could pull back even more, and maybe that would also cause her to not take you so for granted, because you're not engaged within the typical push-and-pull that it has been in this lifetime with her.

"And then you're staying in your center, rather than coming out of your center in reaction to her forcing her worldviews onto you and how *you*, her daughter, need to be. But instead, you're not triggered by her dominating behavior, you're engaged in more self-care and self-nurturance and self-love, which will cause her to peak her little eyes up over the brick wall like Humpty Dumpty and curiously come over more to your side, wondering what you're up to. Your typical flow of energy has been removed, pulled back to *your* center, and you've created space for her now to come forward, because for one, she's wondering where you've gone energetically, and two, that frequency of love, whether for self or other, speaks louder than anything else. So she'll smell this out and respond to it."

"Okay. I got it!"

"And then you'll also need to visualize some type of material, whether rubber or silicon or whatever, that is all around you in a bubble that she can't get through. So when you're there, and when you're with your dad, too, their mayhem won't be absorbed by your third chakra, where the empathic equipment exists, and you won't be sucking in their anxiety, leading you to lay in bed last night feeling anxious for the first time ever. And it's such progress that you *knew* instantly this was your mother's anxiety, not yours, and that it caused you to feel so drained, because that's also where our intimate relationships cord is, so folks whom we're in relationship with, if they suck our power, it's from there, the power center for the chakra system — right?"

"Yup. Drained. Weird that it's both where I suck in energy and it's where I get my power."

"Ah, you're such a good student!" I said with a smile in my tone so she could hear the humor. "But it's true! There's that divine sense of humor — the cosmic joke or the divine comedy as many have called it — at play, exemplified by this razor's edge of where our potential weakness is and also where our potential strength is. It's what we're doing together — rewiring your foundational energy patterns so that your subconscious and unconscious beliefs cause the chakras to be in their balanced state, clearing out where up until now they have shown up as your weakness, and turning them into your strength. You see this, and that takes an advanced understanding."

"I do see it and wow! This is such fun! I never knew life could be like this. That there were other options to the way I was living my life!"

This is the main reason I do what I do.

What else is possible?

And as of now, my recently concluded *Your Sensitivity Is Your Power* telecall series includes this exact retraining. My vibrant team and I are in the midst of making this telecall series available to all through my website. In call number three you can hear and feel the massive shift(s) out of the pattern of taking in and on too much of others' stuff through the third chakra being rewired, into now it being restored as your power center. That was an absolutely fun and brilliant telecall series, with the folks reporting such increases in ease, joy, and freedom from releasing feelings of heaviness and burden—especially with others' stuff—that I ended up in tears and a smile earlier today, speaking with one of the participants.

This telecall series goes into the three or four foundational energy patterns through the main chakras involved with having learned unconsciously to take on or absorb others' energy—and particularly the negative—in an unconscious effort to help those we love feel better. I highly recommend this for everyone who feels the Yes here.

And I say, "Welcome to your new life."

That is what is possible with this kind of work. When we take what has been previously operating within us at an unconscious and subconscious level due to beliefs we are not even consciously aware of but that are very much still running the show with what choices we do and don't make—and especially where we keep ourselves locked into one way of living because we simply don't consider much outside of what we've seen and experienced, and have heard others around us who are like us have seen and experienced—then that becomes our freedom to truly begin to live from our Yes! We can seek what else is possible, beyond our current level of wellness and thriving in mind, body, spirit, finances, and joy in creating our finances, relationships—all aspects of our lives. This is where we now begin to enter into thriving.

And this is where the brave ones, the advanced ones, who have that knowing inside of them—like you reading this now—are able to go.

Advanced

Chapter Five

Replacing Forcing and Efforting with Allowing and Receiving

Cause is effect concealed, and effect is cause revealed.

~ Vimalananda

"I just have to figure it out."

I had been back from Asia for just one year when I began to hear my clients and students say this. I have been meditating for so long (twenty-three years) and had just returned from such a different living environment and cultural milieu, that at first I didn't register what they were really saying when saying, "I just have to figure it out." I hadn't said that for decades and hadn't heard it for at least a decade. So I no longer had any resonance with it, and therefore didn't recognize what they were saying to me with such intimate familiarity for them.

I remember quite clearly the first time I heard one of my clients say this. I was tuned into her system in the first fifteen minutes of her ninety-minute session, and she was updating me on all that had gone on since her session the week before, and what she desired from our session that day. As I helped balance her central nervous system and was kneeling down at her toes, I looked up to her strong jawline, framed by blonde hair, and her sturdily built shoulder span—and her talking head that seemed to just be spewing forth energy from her mouth, her head surrounded by a buzz of "dah dah, dah dah" that acted like a rapid, steady pulse as the overall backdrop pounding forth her presence. She was such a force of energy and was becoming increasingly empowered with more vitality activated, having just left her husband after wrestling with him about his addictions for years. She is what would be called *a go-getter* and she was really making things happen for herself. She was into martial arts and had a mind that was quite strong, yet she knew she required some support to bring her system back into balance as she completed the divorce proceedings. And she knew she needed to tame the parts of her mind that were interfering with her belief and her ability to go for more in her life beyond what she'd previously allowed herself to have, be, and live from.

I was actually also assisting her in how to do all this more efficiently, without her—or really, her ego-mind—"just having to figure it out" and approaching all the changes she desired to make for herself and her kids and her business less from a mental sense that brought in the accompanying efforting, forcing things to happen, and controlling it all as it goes step-by-step. The client, let's call her Jess, was wise enough to open up to what else was possible for her, aware that it could be easier, and require less effort—at least since she began working with me.

That in and of itself took quite a few months of hammering back to her foundational energy patterns so invested in struggle and difficulty and having to fight for what she desired—she'd been orphaned as a young girl—the natural energies of peace, calm, ease, and well-being. So as I unwound her old foundational energy patterns out of her chakra system, I paid particular attention to balancing out these energy patterns within the relevant chakras that had been created and conditioned within trauma, pain, and suffering, and then cultivated by the family and societal environment she grew up enmeshed within. One key was rewiring her root chakra's energy patterns for her to feel safe in her body, that there was not a threat of abandonment nor rejection, and that she was wanted — period — without having to put forth extra effort in order to be wanted and loved.

So as we progressed through her transformation, I brought in the element of mindfulness so she could assist this reprogramming within her system by Observing it, creating changed outcomes in her life, and actively choosing changed outcomes for herself. Thus, one of the key areas we worked on was developing the Observer, while unwinding those unconscious and subconscious foundational energy patterns, along with the accompanying body-mind adrenal burnout the stress and incessant fighting for what she wanted had brought on. Jess ultimately became freer and less triggered throughout the separation, then divorce, and the restructuring she desired for her business. Today, she is engaged to a man who adds value to her life, rather than one she has to fight and caretake. She has also left a business partnership that had her fighting for what she wants and has chosen a solo track of business, in which she has created more ease for herself and her financial life.

It was really cool how we set about transforming her — out of her mind-dominant existence and into that of an active chooser of what she wanted in her life. I was able to present life to her in such a way that it began to seem to her as if she were at a buffet. And the sheer joy of having so many more choices available to her — rather than being constricted to only what she'd known and grew up seeing, and was seeing others around her choose — really was exhilarating to support in its growth. It was such joy to free her and watch as she became increasingly enlivened with all that she began to recognize was now opening up and possible for her and her life and her kids' lives. It is such a charmed, elegant process that is loads of fun to open folks up to reaching into the unknown and turning them onto unlimited possibilities, rather than a life of limitation and contraction and settling.

This, as we have seen, is also ripe soil for the ego-mind to take a firm anchor in and dominate. Really, it is one of my greatest honors and sheer joys to turn folks on to living beyond their minds, and from the mystical, or multidimensional realms of the juiced-up lives we're really meant to be here choosing and creating and living—when in alignment with that quieter, eternal part of ourselves. But that ego-mind is so darn loud, and as it still stands today, in such need to retain its primary positioning as the most valued commodity—a strong mind with a fully developed intellect, and a go-getter personality, all still stemming from the ego-identity—that the quieter, more subtle energies that accompany the sacred parts of existence, where our Higher Selves can be heard and accessed, remain hidden, as if a trick.

Until one wakes up. As has already been discussed, it could be said that what is happening is everyone is being given from their Higher Selves whatever it is they require in their lives to wake up—and then it's a choice whether to wake up through that crisis, difficulty, diagnosis, break-up, or job loss, or not.

But what if it didn't require suffering to do so?

The extra magic behind all this with Jess was during the 2011 and 2012 energies. Considering the backdrop of these new times, where it is not about having to figure it out; make a plan; follow a strategy; and strive toward a goal that remains fixed and unchangeable off in the distance, near or far; or just getting a plan together; it seemed to make even more sense to go *with* the grain of these times, rather than against it. She got this because of her own background in martial arts.

In both my own practice and my teaching of chi gong, the eighteen movements are a great teaching on the universe's natural flows of energy. You just can't argue with the movements and teachings of chi gong; they're so basic to life and able to be seen, that there's just an acceptance that this is the way it is. And then, if one is smart, it's a further learning of how to use these natural flows of energy to one's advantage.

One movement, called *the pushing and pulling of waves*, is one of the most profound for me. It informed my then-already firmly established meditation and yoga practice with a bodily experience of part of what I was re-conditioning myself and my mind and my system to gain from learning to detach from the ego-mind by returning my attention back to my breath. The pushing element of this move is the first half of it and yields a sense of forcing, of going against. The pulling element of this move is the second half, and gives a sense of yielding, of allowing, or receptivity that naturally balances in its opposition to the first half.

It seems this is the nature of what we're talking about here. When we use our minds to go beyond what we've known and create our lives in the ways we desire, truly desire them to be, it is not our minds we're coming from. We are coming from beyond our minds. The joy from something that lights us up involves the heart, which is the major magnetizer and mover of subtle energies of our entire mind-body-spirit system. The Chinese Taoist system recognized that the heart is where the Spirit is located; both share the same word, *shen*, in Chinese. So when we're enjoying what we do, or are in joy, then our Spirit bubbles up more, which brings us into alignment, and that activates more of the subtle energies all around us—the chi, or morphogenic fields—to be more easily moved in the direction of what we're desiring. Hence easier manifestations come for those who are aligned and creating from their joy. This movement of energies that supports us in our co-creation of what we desire to bring forth is a process of elegance and ease. It's one that we have to allow, rather than control. So really, the ironic aspect to observe here contains more of that divine sense of humor, or cosmic joke. The part of us that does the controlling when we live an ego-mind-dominated life is really the part of us that needs to be brought under control by our Eternal Self, or Higher Self, or Observing Self, or Spirit, or however you construe this.

A key question I've asked of my meditation students for decades is: "If, when we're engaged in this meditation practice, we are able to Observe our minds thinking and we're able to pull our attention off our thinking minds and back to our breath, who are we really?

If we are able to rise above, as they say, or be bigger and behind our thinking mind and the incessant thoughts it churns out as it does its job of being the thought factory that it is, then what does that say about the intended rank the mind is delegated to have?

Who is this who is Observing the thinking mind, or your thoughts?

This is your Presence.

So thinking—and then thinking and believing that there is something we have to figure out—are the pushing, the forcing, and the controlling. Being still enough at times in our daily lives (i.e., doing some type of practice), and still enough mentally throughout our lives (so we are Observing ourselves in life, what juices us *and* what makes us both the most excited and a bit trepidatious to really try, so it feels like it's pushing one's edge), this is the allowing part.

I have to insert this now. I have been writing this part at a local park. As I was writing the first bit of the last chapter, I heard a red-tailed hawk cry out and land right on the pine tree limb in front of me, up over my head. It was crying out to another red-tailed hawk behind me. So it was like I was under and within their exchange. The red-tailed hawk symbolizes power and the kundalini awakening. There are a few other meanings I have come to understand the red-tailed hawk has for me, including becoming much more present in my life on a daily basis (no, I did not live near a nest) once I began to use my energy medicine at a more active and focused level.

And just now, as I was writing the part about being still, I looked up and there was a deer looking directly at me from about thirty feet away. After I looked into its eyes — I'm so not making this up — it wagged its tail! And then ran away. Deer symbolize gentleness and unconditional love. I saw a deer as I first drove into this park. My attention was caught so I looked to the left and there it was looking right at me! And this one wagged its tail after I made eye contact with it. I don't really think these two are the same deer. There are a fair number of deer in this park. This existence on a more subtle level really allows for a whole lot more interaction of a more magical existence. But it can't be accessed or usually even noticed from a loud mind that is busy trying to figure out what it needs to do to force, control, and make things happen that it deems are desired, from an ego-identity place, rather than aligned with the more subtle, eternal parts of ourselves. It just stays under the radar of a loud mind and remains hidden.

The allowing is ourselves receiving; therefore, the support naturally aligns with us once we align ourselves, from the subtle energies within us and all around us as the universal life force that it is. And perhaps it's something more—we'll get to this in just a bit. This something more is arrived at only once we've been able to make the mind increasingly serviceable to our overall mind-body-spirit system's genuine desires and alignment, so that the allowing and the receptivity to this allowing and to this increasing support are given a channel on which to get to us. If you're more of a newbie, you may want to reread this last paragraph. So many of these teachings require rereads and repetition.

"Layered and experiential" is what one of my clients recently called it.

This seems like a good spot to mention that I see my clients and students having an increasingly easier time with mindfulness and the cultivation of their Observers. I also hear colleagues speak about seeing this within their client and student base. Perhaps the energies of the cosmos and the progression of this new era of humanity's awakening have hit a threshold with enough of us doing this to now have collapsed the old paradigm vibrationally. Thus it is making the new era's energies more accessible, and in the process, making the mind serviceable, meaning that quieting the ego-mind's demands and control and dominance is becoming easier. Hallelujah to that!

So this means a lot of things, quite frankly. The act of creation is largely different than what we were led to understand about how to take steps toward a goal, as most of us have been conditioned under a social paradigm built under the steadier, more reliable and stable world presented to us within Newtonian physics. An apple drops down from a tree—that is Newtonian physics. We can rely on gravity to show us what is predictable and rely on these physical laws' consistencies and build our lives based on these understandings.

So yes, as I go into depth in my first book, *What if There's Nothing Wrong?* we are now in the age of quantum physics, among other things, and are therefore no longer working, playing, loving, and living with our backdrop being these sturdy universal laws of energy Newtonian physics and a society built on this then created. Linearity, for example, is a lot easier to maintain within a Newtonian physics world: concrete sequential learning and teaching, where first *a* happens, then *b*, then *c*, as in one thing leads to another, one step at a time, and *a* has to be done before *b*, otherwise everything falls apart.

Does this remind you of your daily to-do lists?

Of your business plans?

Action plans for buying that new home?

In this process of having our desires, choices, and creations come into physical form out of energy and into the world of matter, the analytical, factual, and linear mind is not our best friend. But relying on its logic, consider the metaphor of when we're looking to undo a screw and we go to our toolbox and grab a wrench. It just simply is not the right tool. We create from emotion and feeling and tone behind whatever desires we have, especially when we're functioning with an opened, awakened, flowing chakra system. So the life in which we're living our days full of the energies of what we've been desiring and saying yes to and taking only inspired action toward is not gotten to through the analytical mind. It is gotten to more by our energies, our emotions, and our tone all interacting to create a certain frequency that emits from us and brings a matching frequency in whatever shows up.

The mental blocks that get in the way here at first are the analytical mind wanting to understand and chew it apart as it does. Then there are the lockdowns in energy as the unconsciousness and subconscious blocks stemming from our hidden beliefs and previous traumas. These can have us blocking our allowance of what we desire aligning to us because we're not that frequency-emitting station, so to speak.

So beyond the mind and its subconscious beliefs, and beyond the unconsciousness that can become entangled into blocks to the flow of energy residing first within the relevant chakra the beliefs are correlated to and then out into the body as a whole, is the possibility of a super-charged system. There is so much to the desire, and to the choice made from our own free will, and then the continued choice to allow the universe to do what it does in the act of creation, and we *get out of the way* of this creation. This getting out of the way that leads us to creating ananda is more an act of allowing. Rather than the forcing, the efforting, and the diligence that at some point becomes control and struggle, to be effective co-creators in today's world requires our Awakened Presence. This Presence then has the necessary vibrations to its consciousness to engage the universe on our behalf, as we have yoked ourselves with the universe, via our Higher Self, our Awakened Presence. This yoking — the meaning of *yoga* is to *yoke* our individual consciousness, our Higher Self, to the universe's flow of consciousness — allows, yes, but also goes so far as to *invite* the universe to be our co-creator. This then creates the pathway for the universe yoked with our Higher Self to deliver to us what we've attuned to and aligned ourselves with via our desire of what to create.

So is this not a setup for us to be able to create our bliss?

In a culture that glorifies the intellectual mind and the achievements that stem from it, this concept at first seems counterintuitive to many.

Questions such as: "Well, if I'm doing nothing, then nothing will happen?"

And doesn't all success that stems from our continued perseverance require continued effort, especially when things get hard?

So don't I need to keep at it with this level of zeal and pushing?

And how do I just sit back and allow the universe to come in and make anything happen?

But remember, this is also happening in a milieu where subtle energies are not valued. So you have this external reality and its paradigm having conditioned you, pushing in on you while you're choosing with courage to follow your inner knowing. It may not be the easiest thing for you at first. But just like with meditation, over time (or quite quickly; you decide) you develop the musculature from the practice of redirecting your attention and energies in a certain direction while *not* allowing them to go in another direction. Gather the support both internally and externally for your envisioning and your alignment and your choices to feel good and have more juice in your life as they begin to take on a life of their own. Meanwhile you are guided to come out of this conditioning because you sense there's more to it than just what is shown to us as possible in that reality's paradigm.

Within a quantum-physics worldview, that slow, steady pace isn't our backdrop anymore. And you can look at the Internet and how that has created, as it is vastly used today, exponentialized outcomes that were once limited by time and space. So these two factors—quantum physics as the new science informing our times and the Internet 2.0—really mirror each other quite succinctly in all that is becoming available now.

Quantum physics, as the primary science that informs us of how the physical universe is understood to exist now, is a science based on the understanding that our physical universe has a lot in common with consciousness. There are not yet clear statements coming out of orthodox science that assert this so clearly, but there are increasing studies being done on the effects of thoughts, consciousness, and the mind-body connection, which are then able to be seen as mirroring how we're discovering the universe works. So while things are only just barely beginning to be built into the social structures and institutions and economy, as our society is still learning what this means and what these new institutions and social structures and paradigm overall need, it is still influencing how each of our minds are operating.

Let's now add in the very big factor that will help you with that last statement: we have entered into Humanity's Spiritual Awakening. I have spent quite a lot of time and energy teaching and speaking on how this is showing up in my clients, students, and my colleagues' clients and students, my friends, and myself. I am a naturalist scientist, as yogis are taught to be. I observe for my guiding truths; I don't just make claims based on passed-down or conditioned beliefs. And what I'm seeing is that people's brains do not function in the same way. People's bodies are showing weird symptoms that when they go to their primary care doctor, or emergency room, the tests come back as if nothing is wrong. There is no explanation for their heart palpitations, as if living in perpetual excitement. Or there is not a cause to point to why they have begun to have their vision affected, in that they're seeing more trailers of lights go by, as if there are holes in what they're perceiving every now and again.

There are. The veils are thinning. The Mayans built those pyramids—triangular stone structures—to help the earth harness the high frequencies predicted to be showered down upon earth in the 2012 timing. I observed my bare feet on the Earth when I was there on 12/21/12 tingling with electricity, whereas the year before when I'd gone, not at all.

There have been major astrological and astronomical events that if you were to go on nasa.com or space.com and review the list of the various planetary alignments and activities just since 12/2012, you'd begin to notice the statement: "And something like this only happens every five hundred years; this is the very same configuration that happened when Jesus was born (star of Bethlehem, spring 2015); when this configuration last occurred, it was when Israel became a nation," and on and on to the point that it would simply be naive to not take notice.

Just yesterday in a workshop I facilitated for students of my energy medicine and of any energy medicine, fellow facilitators in consciousness, as we looked at the nature of what energy and consciousness has been like to work with over the past month, I said that there is a reason why there are so many new folks wanting to learn about these practices, wanting to learn yoga and meditation, taking to eating cleaner food and demanding our food supply be cleaned up from the industrial food revolution that has done what it has done with the additives. People are waking up because this is the Awakening time, the greatest leap in humanity's evolution, our Spiritual Awakening. And increasingly we are seeing the effects of what this means. But there is no plan that is marked down for us on how to move through the effects of these high energies showering down onto our planet and affecting our brains' wirings, our central nervous systems, our structural alignment, our hormonal systems' balance, and our subtle bodies' expressions.

Since 2010 I have increasingly listened for guidance. The guidance I receive occurs from listening within when in meditation, when out under the night sky, and when in session with clients who present me with their systems' reactions to these energies.

The bottom-line question seems to be: "What is this all about—the nature of our times and these changed vibrations and energies that I and others sense?"

I also speak with others who are asking—and that's now you too.

Those who know and love me have heard one of my mantras: *I don't have to be right. I have to be happy.*

So please take what is presented here to you—as I know you know, but it's a reminder—and let it speak to your own knowing. In the yogic tradition, there is a deep history of taking in the wisdom gained from a teacher, and then seeing how and if it applies to our own individual systems. So let yourself become that Observer even more, not just for the increased mindfulness, but also to see what you're able to pick up on the nature of these changes presenting to us all. This is a moment-by-moment navigation compared to what it was like up until and around 2010. Yes, even with the 2008 economic crash, which many say was a part of this reshuffling in which we're moving into a new world, based on new systems and structures sprouting forth from their grounding in these new energies of Oneness. In numerous different studies, quantum physics has shown that everything is interrelated — that we are more about collaboration, community, cooperation, inclusiveness, and harmony. These are all higher levels on the vibrational scale of emotions and actions, likened to the Higher Self version of ourselves, and not as aligned anymore with the ego-mind-created emotions and structures of competition, seclusion, divide and conquer, and self-serving pursuits from the old economy.

Because it seems, indeed, what people are coming to me for the most often is to align themselves and their lives with what we might call their *authenticity*. Authenticity is the buzzword, but when I think of an authentic person, I think of one who listens less to the false voices of the ego-mind, based in fear and lack, and one who is listening more, choosing, and acting from the Higher Self version, or the Awakened Self, or the — yes, I'm going to say it — Spiritualized Self.

The chakra column is a really vigorous, tight, succinct, and reliable road map for this awakening process. And again here I am not speaking to the more advanced kundalini rising or awakening, but to the lighter process of having one's body, mind, and spirit integrated fully into the buzzing, awakened system of humming life force that invigorates and informs all aspects of our lives. What we're really talking about here is an increase in one's light. To awaken to and then awaken one's own vital life force is another way to become en-lightened, rather than closed down, without consciously accessing and utilizing this life force. If vital life force energy, or chi or prana, is electric and magnetic — as it has been shown to be — then this has a frequency, or wattage, or Hz.

And this is why I choose the words buzzing and humming.

What do we convert electricity into?

Light. When people's unconscious beliefs weigh them down and stop them from opening further in their lives and expanding, then their systems are not circulating as much chi or prana as they could, so they're carrying and circulating and accessing less chi or prana—or light. Think of how you feel when you're happy and when you're depressed.

Which one is lighter?

There again, pay attention to the subtle and value it for the information it in fact is.

Why would we overlook something that is so innately our own, naturally wired into our existence?

Emotions are no small part of our lives, yet we have relegated them to the irrational realms rather than look to them for the wisdom and guidance and portal into how we're really doing and what we're really believing. Then we could make adjustments accordingly, which would eventually show up as inspired, informed action.

This then clears blocks in the chakras as we reach beyond our outdated state of living once aware—or conscious—of our emotional and mental entanglements. Thus, more chi or prana is able to flow throughout our systems. And we thus have greater access to more energy, inner wisdom, intuitive guidance, and inspired action that is in alignment with our Higher Selves and not our Lower Selves' fears. It is cyclical; the more activated we become, more accessible are the increasing levels of intuitive guidance, life force, the more our alignment increases, the more we're taking inspired action, the more the alignment increases, and the more supportive events line up externally. This, too, has momentum. The momentum goes either way. Like attracts like.

However, this goes beyond the chakra column. We don't need to limit what is going on here to one structure. It is universal, as is the chakra system's wisdom in its guidance provided from being the treasure map it is to human awakening, well-being, vitality, and thriving in mind, body, and spirit. But we don't need to limit the way we go about our awakening process to just the chakra column and system.

All animate life has chi flowing through it. All chi, to me, has become invigorated with this new awakened light in response to these energies pouring down on our planet, including the Earth itself. So whatever is going to assist you in wrapping your brain around living your life in alignment with your Presence — your Higher Self being the leading force in your life, with your Lower Self seeded in the ego-mind successfully managed from your practices — *that* is what we're talking about.

Living a life of alignment means we're opened, listening, and receiving. It's our antenna strengthening and our perceptibility increasing what our antennas are picking up, so we can live in tune with what is going on, not in resistance. The ego-mind typically creates this with its fear-based focus on separation, lack, and unworthiness, which manifests in a host of different destructive thoughts and behaviors.

Living an opened life, where we're receptive to the flow of life, means we're *allowing* rather than *forcing*. It's a balanced energy flow of both the masculine energies of the active, yang forces and the feminine energies of the passive, yin forces. Where we recognize that before anything becomes manifest in the physical, it is 99 percent vibrational first. As I said over and over again in *What if There's Nothing Wrong?*, where the recognition of where our power really lies, as it is so wisely construed in the East, is in the subtle. And so this subtle energy is focused within the feminine energies.

What does this cool yoga- or chi-gong-like phrasing mean?

That we're attenuating to the subtle energies, working with and cultivating ourselves and our creations at these seed-and-watering levels before they ever break through the physical soil and become carrots or sunflowers. Our thoughts, emotions, and energy levels are key to informing us of what we're creating.

Another key informing us is the fifth chakra, which is about the strength of our creative capacities released and realized within our own systems and working in our favor with what we're creating as our lives. Yes, the fifth chakra is about more than the communication aspects, which are most frequently focused on when an easy, cursory explanation is provided. This is the seat of choice, and in the last five years, my clients have required their throat chakras worked with—surrounding 2012—more than I ever have before in twenty years of practice. I have not been looking for it; I couldn't obtain the results for my clients that I get if I went in with my mind concluding that I know what they need. Rather, I listen to their systems as they present to me where they would like the focus. And then the wisdom of their systems and the innate intelligence of the energy I'm working with take over, as the life force that they are.

Client after client, when they present to me, require focus on the throat chakra. Whether an actual physical issue of a chronically tight neck or tight upper shoulders, chronic sore throat or a thyroid issue or a seemingly inexplicable loss of voice when one has gone for every test imaginable, this is all indicated within the fifth chakra. It also includes those feeling restricted and having little to no choice in their lives, or lacking courage to go for and actively choose to have and create in their lives what they're genuinely desiring rather than settling. Three words: creation, choices, courage—these are the key to becoming who it is we are most aligned with being and becoming in our lives.

I have a client, let's call her Mary. Her three daughters have grown up referring to her as Mary Poppins, in fact, so this feels like a good pseudonym. Mary is in her early seventies, although that wouldn't really occur to you as you talk with her. Of the past six years, she has spent five of them taking care of her aging, ailing mother. Her mother died this past March. Mary got a virus last October, in what was the last of her five years taking care of her mother. What was happening was that she was increasingly drained from this. As much as she loved and cherished her mother and had spent five years feeling increasingly locked into this duty without question, she was not eating life-force-giving foods. She simply hadn't learned the "stay away from anything with fat in it, and go for the low-fat foods," which was a diet fad in the 1980s. That fad led to people eating food with more additives to make up for the reduced fat, and therefore reduced flavor. All combined, this threw her system into what is known as chaos, which replaced her natural state of homeostasis. Another way to say it is that the toxic load tipped out of her favor.

Notice that all of what was just described was in the subtle energies and requires attention geared to the levels of vitality, stress, emotional robustness, quality of sleep, and food. Exercise, too, because that releases mostly life force, health-giving biochemical responses. This is not a place for the personal trainer to go into any kind of discussion of the type of exercise, but just in case you're thinking it—there you go.

Mary's system became weakened overall, and the vulnerability showed up in the chakra most related to the domains of her life that were tipping her system out of homeostasis—feeling restricted, without choice, limited, not having the courage to choose differently, and possibly not having the courage to speak up about her genuinely increasing feelings of burden. Mary had been so conditioned to be a good person, was so loving and so nurturing and such a light in her own right, that she believed this simply wasn't what a good, loving person felt! There were also accompanying feelings of guilt and shame, and making herself bad and wrong for feeling this way, which she also kept buried. This affected another chakra, which I worked on to unwind core energetic patterns.

What I have seen among my clients and students is something I've not heard any other practitioner versed in the chakra system talk about. Usually the fifth chakra is presented as the one dealing with communication, and I've found that too, yes. But there is another level to the fifth chakra that I've seeing increasingly over the past five years, which I've had to piece together myself as a more current aspect of the fifth chakra. This is so much so that I've been saying recently that this is the chakra of our times.

Much of this seems due to the fact that the neck can act as a bottleneck or a bridge for the Higher Self's guidance and wisdom that shower in from above, or from our crown chakra, or from our connection to Source. This depends on how we construe the way we receive our guidance and connection to a Source bigger than us, whether it's non-spiritualized chi or a yoking with the divine force within us and from which we are connected. Remembering that *yoga* in Sanskrit translates into *to yoke with* in English, its implied meaning is to yoke with this divine source through the practices outlined within yoga: meditation, poses, cleansing kriyas, prana, and chi-moving pranayama, awareness, and activation of the chakras. These help us better contextualize what I'm presenting here and now and understand it. We're no longer talking about folks being able to live in ashrams and dedicate their lives to their spiritual practices, or off in a mountain meditating in a cave. Now it's about being awakened, enlightened beings here in our post-modern, globalized lives of today, within all that we are being, producing, and doing. It looks a bit different than the ancient wisdom presented at times, and yet it is quite practical and applicable to today's times, if understood appropriately. In fact, the ego-mind—so cultivated by these post-modern, globalized, commercialized times—is so in need of a check that these practices are central to us moving beyond our previous limitations of the old and into this new era, thriving in ways that combine ancient wisdom with post-modern creativity.

Returning to the chakra system, the next chakra down from the crown and one up from the throat is the third eye. I'm referring now to the energy medicine that I created, Vibrational UPgrade energy medicine, and how the chakras flow energy within each chakra and therefore regions of our bodies and relevant domains of life (i.e., love, communication, creativity, sensuality) and ultimately our entire chakra column as a complete unit. This includes our entire body from head to toe and all of our invisible, subtle energy bodies that emanate out from and meet at each of the seven main chakras. When that's complete, what we have is a robust ability to create a life that we desire with ease, well-being, vitality, love, abundance, confidence, clarity, centeredness, connection to our true feelings, ability to speak of our true feelings, and an overall hearty, full, awakened life in a body pulsing with vital life force energy, so it is supple, strong, and vibrant, and age is irrelevant. Key to this is feeling that all of life is lived from choice, and not any sense of restriction or limitation, whether recognized as self-created through unconscious or subconscious blocks, or perceived as external hindrances to our freely choosing what we desire to create.

The symbolism for the third eye chakra, located directly above the throat chakra, shows up in cultures all over the world. The blue eye that is sold everywhere in Istanbul is from this connection and is used to "protect against someone invading our seeing eye." This intuitive seeing, understood as a power throughout ancient and into modern-day cultures globally, is the sixth chakra, aka, "the third eye." This intuitive seeing helps to, in a sense, interpret the guidance and wisdom from our connection to something bigger than us. This guidance is meant to assist us, now, in seeing how our own innate being and gifts can contribute to the world today and help us create brilliant, awakened lives. The chakra beneath it, the throat chakra, is the lever, so to speak, that allows for this guidance to drop down more toward the manifesting and physical chakras, assisting us with the courage to choose to create our lives. And when we stay jammed up in doing this, then we feel it very much in the throat chakra.

We are being asked to acknowledge our co-creative powers now. In quantum physics' view of the world, we are living in an energy soup. Our thoughts that we think continuously—not randomly here and there, those "floaters" as I have come to call them—create a neurological groove so that it's easier to continue to think these thoughts and ancillary thread of similar thoughts. This then contributes to creating a certain momentum and tone, which becomes one of our predominant vibrations.

At this point, it is helpful then, when considering the universal law of magnetism, aka law of attraction, to be mindful of what is creating our predominant vibrations, yes? Like attracts like. This momentum of thinking these kinds of thoughts makes it easier and easier to think and end up back there in those thoughts and wake up within these types of thoughts. At that point, we're calling to us matching vibrations from the world around us, based on the law of magnetism (LOA or Law of Attraction also describes this).

We can also use this momentum, this magnetism, to our advantage. And this is why I have taken the time to write this book. I write this within the partial solar eclipse, the full supermoon lunar eclipse with the autumn equinox and the gamma rays of an exploding star, all showering upon us. There has been an opening here, in September 2015. There seems to be more support now to acknowledge how we are creating our lives based on our most commonly held thoughts and therefore choices and to pull out of this with the Observer. And also support to then redirect this momentum toward consistently choosing what is in alignment with the most brilliant aspects of ourselves being brought forth and creating much joy for ourselves and for those whose lives we touch, and therefore contribute to.

This does not happen through a step-by-step action plan. Nor does this happen through force and control or efforting. New skills are required in this new paradigm in which to thrive, because it's commanding us to make choices and create thriving lives. So this newness is not approached through the intellectual mind, figuring it all out, with a concrete sequential action plan that we stick to no matter what as our thirteen-step blueprint, or roadmap to success, and thus forcing and controlling the conditions to match what we've compiled from our figuring it out. This ego-mind, or intellectual mind that we're so familiar with, in fact restricts our access to the life force showering down upon us and all around us to assist us with guidance about how to use and apply and respond to these energies that allow us the support from this natural alignment. The ego-mind squeezes us off from this supportive natural flow, where we're separated from the flow of the vital life force energies, and thus have to then force and control and make things happen.

The mind has to be reeled in and made serviceable. It was a good tool for the old paradigm, but this new one isn't about the ego-based, personality-based, identity-based self. And that's where our ego-mind's fear-based thoughts stem from, because its job is to protect us. This includes the shielding us from the new and the unknown until it can be labeled, evaluated, judged, and filed away as "this is that." But as we continue to evolve in this time of humanity's greatest leap in evolution, it seems that part of what is evolving is this very wiring within us that once favored the ego-mind and glorified the power of the intellectual mind's capacities. What we looked to for measures of success and source of the measurable, material outcomes of this success is no longer what is in favor. If we are not choosing to expand our lives, as all of nature does if you look at trees and flowers and kids, and instead remain in the cozy kingdom the ego-mind keeps us contained in, with its preference for the status quo because it already understands it, then we will have less access to the juice of life, the life-force current.

The nature of our times is in fact containing thrusts of energy supporting us to live in our most blissed-out state, while fully embodied, creating work, relationships, homes, and communities that are in that alignment with our Inspired Selves. It seems, from what I've noticed from the sheer volume of people seeking my work, that people's suffering is increased until and so that they do something to move beyond their status quo — forced by circumstances or such discomfort that they then grudgingly see about what needs to change.

Instead, replacing this are the capacities of the heart and an awakened mind. Here, living in alignment with the nature of our times and within our own system's optimal functioning, the lower mind has been reined in and made increasingly serviceable. This allows for more fertility within our overall receptivity to our guidance pouring through about how to create, and what to choose, and intuitively inspired actions at just the right time. One step at a time.

And these steps are inspired by the guidance of what is now picked up on in that moment, or on that day, depending on how things have proceeded, rather than a mandated, stasis action plan that is forced to be made to happen regardless of the responses and reshuffling within the environment that we interact with. Forcing and efforting actually increase resistance to allowing what we want to show up. This is the nature of the movement into an era based on spiritual juice and quantum physics, and less on Newtonian physics and the intellectual mind and its pursuits.

This agility to assess by listening to our guidance, reassessing and then readjusting with the most up-to-date response to what we are focusing on creating, is able to be more responsive. It is also more focused within the subtle behaviors of the feminine, so that the masculine focus on action is not optimal. In fact, the creation or implementation of an action plan is not optimal, because creation with action, without first the requisite attunement within, is like shooting a nonexistent arrow out of one's very real bow at a very real target. Nothing lands, nothing sticks, and nothing hits the target.

When we use ineffective tools for the job at hand, then we are left with results we don't like. This can build frustration into the process, which can grow within the person, obviously. But the information is wrong. It's not the outside world that is not delivering the outcome, based on our functional action plan. When we're listening to our guidance, we're able to assess what will create more, and sense what will create less. So we're creating and choosing, and then taking inspired action based on our tuning into the subtle energies of both the conditions we're looking to affect, and our own levels of ease, joy, and well-being.

If we're feeling frustrated, then something we're doing is not working. Allowing the frustration to inform us, we can see that something is off. We're naturally built to be happy, smiling beings—unless something is wrong. A baby cries when hungry, has poo in his diapers, or is tired. All these responses are signaling to Mom and Dad that something is needed.

Adults are no different (teens a little, ha ha; well, their developmental process does in fact make their guidance system a tad bit less reliable). We can consider any of the less-desirable emotions as markers of when we're off or out of alignment. When we're criticized, that doesn't feel good. When someone is mean to us, that doesn't feel good. Let's leave out the discussion of, "Well, if one grew up getting abused, then criticism and meanness is what is most familiar and in fact is what one then construes as love" for now and just go with the example of a balanced, cleared system. Criticism or meanness does not feel good. This is a marker that we are out of our natural state, or alignment. Otherwise it'd feel good, like riding a bicycle when age eight, or having Mom comfort us when our knee got scraped. We recognize signs and the tones of love. That is our natural state. So that when we're receiving some form of this, we are calmed, soothed, comforted, smiling, relaxed, healthy, and well. But when not feeling this way, these emotions are indicators that something is off. Test this for yourself.

Furthermore, our command over the life force in all of life is reduced drastically when we're perpetually in the range of negative emotions more often than not. Try this—it's from my teaching chi gong to middle school kids. I took them outside and had them watch as I walked by a row of bushes and then stood under a tree. I told them to observe the tree's limb most directly over me and the bushes begin to wave as though in a slight breeze, while the higher branches did not. It was not caused by external factors like wind, but instead could be observed as a response to my field of awakened life force interacting with the awakened life force of the tree and bushes. So the slight breeze began—nowadays it actually typically grows into something quite full! It's brilliant! The leaves were softly waving, while the tree limb itself had slight movement.

When I walk outside now, as I said, the soft wave of hello from our interacting fields can grow into a full breeze. Part of my process within my own mindfulness has been a learning curve. First: "Oh, okay. I can choose my thoughts. Wow!"

And then second: "Oh, okay, so if I can choose my thoughts, why in the world would I choose to listen to this thought that makes me feel like a puddle of mud?"

And then third: "Yes! I choose to feel good. So does this thought make me feel good? Okay, then, go with it!"

The more I've done this through the years, the more that gentle waving of the trees' leaves has grown into full-on breezes. In fact, sometimes I'll use this as a measure of how much life force I'm flowing in my field around my body.

Feeling good is our natural state. So if we're in our natural state, and our life force is therefore awakened, then it only makes sense that we're more capable of communicating with the life force of the animate life forms in our external environment, including people. After talking with someone who is depressed and complains to you about it, you leave feeling less peppy than if you'd just spoken with someone and mutually expressed gratitude over the sunny day. It's just like that. And building that over time creates a momentum that is able to communicate with—some would say here "have command over"—the energies external to us, so that we actually are living in an aligned state that allows for this "communication" or "exchange" of energy to happen.

Changing how we feel changes the external and how that shows up. It is not, *so not*, the other way around. My thoughts create my external reality and my continued perceptions and interpretations and creations in my external environment. I allow and disallow what may want to get created through me and my own unique brilliant self by fear, mistrusting my guidance, or mistrusting that this bigger life force, whether love or divine or neutral or all of the above, has my back at all times.

An ego-mind made serviceable is so much more than increased memory retention, data recall, and peace and calm. That is just the start. An ego-mind that has been wrangled in and put in the corner and called forth when its skills are required, can then allow for this guidance, this communication, this support to be observed, intuited, and become inspired action, rather than dominate. The ego-mind then gets involved with the inspired action, with the logistics of making that phone call, or getting the directions, or scheduling that event in the calendar.

The less the ego-mind is disrupting the natural state of well-being, the less it is contracting back into fear and thus causing tight muscles, and the more we're able to enhance our lives with these massively supportive energies now.

When creation—whether the launch of a new business, new program, new relationship, new home, or whatever physical result we're going for in our lives—is done with the ease described here, in today's energetic milieu, it is more effective at achieving the results desired. This joy then creates what I've come to term "a back-door approach to quieting the mind." An open, receptive system allows, rather than shuts down. Attuning to one's natural levels of joy and ebullience, to the point of having a sense of buoyancy, is the first order of business here. In fact, there seems to be a conspiracy going on to increase our bliss.

Chapter Six

Allowing, Aligning, and Ananda

> *The principle of energy (shakti), functions as a receptive co-creator of the universe.*
>
> *This reflection is of the potential seed of consciousness (parama-shiva), as the vibration (spanda-shakti) of absolute bliss (ananda).*
>
> ~ Marmashastra
> as compiled by Michael Hamilton, 2011

After the Buddha's final nirvana (his death), five hundred enlightened monks convened a council at Rajagaha for the purpose of collecting all the Buddha's teachings and committing them to memory so they could be handed down to future generations. Because he knew so much dharma, it was essential that Ananda, Buddha's loyal personal attendant, be present— but he was not yet enlightened

While the Buddha was alive, Ananda strove to free the Buddha from as many mundane activities as possible so he could concentrate on teaching the dharma and helping people. To that end, he washed and mended the Buddha's robe, tidied his living quarters, washed his feet, massaged his back, and when he was meditating or talking, Ananda stood behind him, keeping him cool with a fan. He slept near the Buddha so to always be at hand and accompanied him when he made his round of the monasteries.

Although Ananda's main job was to take care of the Buddha's needs, he always had time to be of service to others as well. He would often give talks on dharma and indeed was such a skillful teacher that sometimes the Buddha would ask him to give a talk in his place, or finish a talk that he had begun. Ananda's selflessness expressed itself in three ways: through his service to the Buddha, through his unstinting kindness to his fellow disciples, both ordained and lay, and also to future generations through the crucial role he had to play in the preservation and transmission of the dharma.

Life in the sangha where Ananda lived was not always easy for the nuns. Most monks kept away from them, not wanting to be tempted. Some even discriminated against them. Ananda, on the other hand, was always ready to help them. It was he who encouraged the Buddha to ordain the first nuns. Additionally, Ananda was always ready to give dharma talks to nuns and laywomen and encourage them in their practice, and they in turn often sought him out because of his empathy for them.

So once the Buddha went to "his final nirvana," or died, and Ananda no longer had to look after the Buddha's needs, he had more time to meditate. He began to practice with exceptional diligence, hoping that he could attain enlightenment before the council started. As the time of the council's commencement got closer, he practiced harder and harder. During the evening before the council he sat meditating, convinced that he would not be able to attain enlightenment by the next morning. So he gave up and decided to lie down and sleep. As his head touched the pillow, he became enlightened. Ananda was warmly welcomed at the council the next day.

What if it were that easy?

To be like Ananda and to learn from his example is actually more about choosing what we most desire, what lights us up the most, and what (therefore) is most in alignment with who we really are, with our own uniqueness, and special qualities that are at the same time the valuable contribution we are able to be to humanity. And once we choose this, even more alignment activates within us and with the bigger—most say divine—force(s) that are co-creating with us. When our choices are in this alignment, we do the proverbial "let go and let God."

And what if the letting go doesn't look like the preconceived mental conclusions of full-on detachment once we've chosen what we want?

But instead, it is more of an ongoing attunement to this part within us that knows who we really are, is aware of what really lights us up and those around us, and what our own unique contributions are to be brought forth. As we continue to choose this, one small step at a time, bringing this special product, service, or way of being within our lives, we are already connected to a bigger Source energy, or divinity, and thus, we are attuned to the act of co-creation because of this alignment.

As mentioned before, *yoga* from Sanskrit to English translates as *to yoke with*.

The connotation is "to yoke with the divine source, the eternal source of all life, that is within each of us as that divine spark, and then beyond us, permeating throughout the collective and the universe."

Therefore, we become more connected to that part of us that is tuned into ourselves and Observing ourselves and witnessing our actions and choices and what they each create as the effects in our lives, whether physically tangible or of a more subtle nature, as in our emotional, mental, and physical levels of well-being. When we are tuned in enough to see what truly juices us when we do something, or act in a certain way, or create that type of product or service, this allows for the co-creation of the expansion we actually desire. With this data, we understand that when we feel this type of juice being on and having more than enough vital life force, and passion, and all of life seems to flow to us with ease and joy, then we have the data observed that show us, okay, this is *the* thing. *This* is what causes me to feel the most myself, so let me therefore choose more of this. An essential part of this process is the clearing out and the mental detachment from the old self-sabotaging mental programs and foundational energy patterns that may be the backdrop of a society of people still settling for life as it has been, rather than going for more of what is desired. Meaning, that we are really seeking to move beyond old constructs of what is possible.

One of the key areas in my life over the past five years increasingly — it has in fact always been the way I have lived my life — has been to ask the universe to assist me with reaching into the unknown so that I can really access beyond what I already know is possible, to work with and bring in more of these newer vibrations all around us, which are known to be the nature of these times we're progressively moving into since 2012. These new energies in particular seemed to have been building over the past month or two, in the fall of 2015. It seems that the physical manifestation now of this new life, this new paradigm, this new era for Humanity's Spiritual Awakening, has reached somewhat of a critical mass, or at least initial threshold, in that more folks have awakened. More of these faster, higher frequencies are now permeating our lives to move beyond any previous constructs of what we've thought was possible, into what feels like an entirely unknown to us level of ease, abundance, well-being, joy, and a whole lot more yet to be revealed. But one major aspect of these new times really feels like it's coming out of the addiction to suffering and struggling.

It seems that, as more of the areas where folks have the most strongly held unconscious beliefs around where suffering and struggling happens in their lives, these areas are being brought forward for release from the struggle. But it could seem like more of a struggle as this cycle peaks in order to be released. This is a natural homeopathic aspect to natural healing. It also seems to be a natural aspect of living life from duality.

So I have been asking, "What else is possible here?"

What would it take for this transition to be had with more ease, comfort, grace, and well-being than we have previously allowed?

Because this connection to the Source energy that is so increasingly prolific and accessible on our planet now has indicated to me in a multitude of ways that struggle and suffering are a choice.

But as the masses have yet to understand this Great Shift that is going on, we seem to be engaged still in the ego-mind's focus on what is difficult, serious, hard, not working, and what causes suffering. This then seems to perpetuate itself. Another main contributing factor — within at least the commercialized, post-modern lifestyle that has a central component on advertising and marketing — is the focus on problems. Marketing 101 teaches companies to present a problem and its services or products as a solution. This is white noise, quintessentially, and at such an unconsciously accepted level that it has infused mainstream thinking in an insidious way.

Replacing a life ruled by the ego-mind and its focus on struggle, the act of co-creation when we are in alignment shows itself to be a natural, elegant, effortless series of choices. The doing of that thing—let's say creating bright textiles with sacred symbols for people to hang in their homes or offices—that makes us feel the most on and full of life, and the Observing of how life shows up all around us, to us, and through us via the people, the events, and how they line up, the increased possibilities and opportunities to bring this aspect of ourselves (i.e., our sacred textiles) more forward, front and present in our lives, all increase our continued choosing of this. We become more *on* and alive, claiming our joy and happiness and abundance that are naturally occurring from doing this thing. All this feeds on itself, building momentum. We notice, or Observe, the act or behavior or creation of that thing that has us the most on and we choose it because it is a natural desire for us and is in fact what causes us to feel so alive. This choice sends out from our emitting frequencies as the collection of thoughts, feelings, emotions—or consciousness. And these frequencies magnetize back to us more of the same.

But there is an additional aspect here, beyond the universal law of magnetism, LOA, or the Law of Attraction. When we choose something based on our desire, and it is aligned with being a contribution to our lives, then our Higher Self's presence is expanding within and around our physical bodies, thus permeating our lives with this sacred Presence due to our choosing expansion. When we increasingly choose this way of life and being from this more sacred space, infused with the guidance from our eternal selves and Source, we have activated more support due to our very alignment. It is the exact opposite

Allowing, Aligning, and Ananda 143

of clinging to the status quo, as our ego-mind prefers and encourages us to do. Living life from the mind shows up as colder, slower, denser energies and texture of living, where there is force, control, and efforting involved in making things happen, simply because what we are doing is from a stance of non-expansion, of resistance to expansion. Then this resistance permeates all aspects of our lives, and we stay in resistance. So this too is momentum. Ananda had to let go of this forcing to make enlightenment happen, choosing to allow it to occur instead, in order for the divine co-creation to come in with his enlightenment. Here, Ananda activated the momentum for his deepest desire, having much support through the council convening and the opportunity to assist with the honoring of Buddha's teachings, something Ananda was deeply connected to from decades of following his bliss. But once he began to push rather than trust and allow, as he continued to fervently meditate right up to the day before the council convened, he activated those energies of the ego-mind. At that point, he chose to let go, rather than clinging and hanging on even tighter with even more force and control, say by perhaps staying up all night meditating. He chose, instead, to surrender from within his overall alignment of his choice and desire, allowing for the co-creation, and voilà! In came exactly what he desired, once he identified that he was forcing and controlling from the ego-mind rather than trusting and allowing from his alignment and the momentum of his previous choices.

And so it is this support that then causes our aligned choices to seem to create such ease in the creation of our lives, gradually, one step at a time from this supportive, collaborative, co-creative positioning. It frequently shows up as friends or relatives who some may be jealous of due to how seemingly easily they create success in their lives. What is being said here is that there is an actual observable science to this act of co-creating, where we make things easier for ourselves because we're living in the alignment that more easily invites in the supportive universal energies to then assist us with physically manifesting this desire. This seems to be the nature of what folks on the cutting edge of this new era are being asked to test and learn—how to work with the natural subtle energies to support and enhance our creations from our aligned desires, rather than remain limited and constricted, settling for life as it has been presented to us as what is possible and figuring out how to make things happen.

Isn't that what Ananda did?

In his overall process, we can see that he first chose, based on his huge love and enthusiasm for Buddha's teachings, to be a part of the council to create the system that would allow Buddha's sacred teachings that had so inspired Ananda to be passed on to future generations. Now, it is worth noting that this is based on what Ananda had been choosing for quite a while prior to Buddha's death and the council convening to preserve Buddha's teachings. He'd already established momentum with his enthusiasm for decades of choosing to support and assist in bringing forth Buddha's teachings. Thus, he was already living in alignment with what he'd found his most enthusiastic and natural Yes to. And then he came up against the possible obstacle of not attaining enlightenment. And he chose to do whatever he could to get himself enlightened before the council convened so he could become a contributing member of this most important task, as he saw it. Somewhere along the line, it seems part of this teaching is that Ananda became so attached to the outcome of enlightenment, due to his intense desire to be a part of the council to preserve his most sacred Master's teachings, that he became a bit more involved in the ego-mind. He seemed to drop his trust a bit with the increased fervency of his dedication and seemed to push more. Yet it can also be said that maybe he was just so focused and intent on choosing his desire that he enthusiastically did all he could do to align himself with what would create the Yes! to his becoming enlightened so he could be a part of the council.

However, the diligence of his practice—"he practiced harder and harder" and the aspect of his finally "giving up" and "deciding to lie down"—seems to imply a certain level of force and control that was unnecessary, that could have been replaced by his alignment and therefore allow the co-creative forces to assist.

He went to sleep in this fervent, dedicated state, and as soon as his exhausted head hit the pillow—no doubt from all the forcing, control, and efforting—he became enlightened. Once he chose ease and knocked out his conscious mind—or his interfering ego-mind—and went to sleep, voilà! He had his goal attained. It's quite telling for me to note here that when I am doing clearings on clients, students, and participants on the Tuesday night group call, many times they knock out and go to sleep when I've hit a big chunk of unconscious or subconscious beliefs.

As we say in the field and I say to them, "It's because I've hit your stuff."

At times the ego-mind can most certainly interfere rather than be the supportive tool (no pun intended) it is meant to be, to assist us in navigating the physical plane through our five senses safely and successfully. This I have found to be where the unconscious and subconscious come into play with their conditioned way of believing, choosing, and behaving. And this is where I do my work with my energy medicine on behalf of clients who come to me seeking an easier way.

When choosing what makes us feel the most on, it expands our aliveness, and thus our vital life force energy is honored. If we don't choose what makes us feel on and alive, it suppresses our vital life force juice in a way that suppresses our own vital life force energy. So we end up with less energy and feel more exhausted and lethargic and *not on* throughout all aspects of our lives. It is cyclic, and it is based on momentum. Yet you can start small, one choice at a time, and notice what these choices then create for the level of juice within you and your life. And then notice the level of supportive synchronicities that seem to occur as all the various aspects required to come together for your success in building more of this energy in your life line up, or also come into alignment. I have come to think of it as living within divine order, a natural order, from our eternal being, rather than living in disorganized chaos, without the natural, co-creative forces built into our very existence collaborating with us, simply because we're not collaborating on our own behalf. Instead, we're choosing against ourselves.

I have come to do increasingly more clearings for my Tuesday night group call subscribers around the unconscious and subconscious blocks of allowing themselves to choose what it is they really desire. It seems the greater backdrop that the masses are engaged with is not feeling free to choose what it is they really desire. Furthermore, it seems like when asked, without bringing forth what it is they don't want, it befuddles more folks than not when asked what it is they actually do desire—if they could have or create or be anything. With the greater backdrop of our global society being composed of the masses, people live their lives from the expectations they've chosen to accept and have been projected onto and into their lives, rather than living from what listening and Observing their own system yields.

It requires some consistent reconditioning for folks to believe that they actually *can* have, create, and be what they desire. The reconditioning I have therefore increasingly seen within my Tuesday night call participants is of steady clearings around all sorts of nuanced beliefs inherited from living in a world still full of people compromising and settling for a life based on their ego-mind's perceived limitations as to what is truly available to them to choose from and to create. This ranges from the influence infused into their conditioning that somehow, because the majority aren't living their lives in ways that their Higher Selves guides them to choose, that they each must therefore not deserve to have what they most desire. They don't feel they deserve having their own inner guidance being there to support them or that they can rely on their guidance and the universe to collaborate with them as they do step out and choose based on their innermost, enthusiastic desires.

These innermost, enthusiastic desires that are most aligned within oneself do contribute to others' lives expanding. This is simply because when we are choosing what makes our hearts open and feel full of meaning and life, then it naturally isn't going to be something that would hurt anyone; otherwise, it wouldn't line up. Further, it could be—but is not necessary—that it is an act that involves service or actively contributing to others' lives, because just by being that *joy* vibration of being so *awake* and *alive* and *on*, we are emitting this vibration, or frequency, to those around us. And we're also contributing to the collective energy soup that exists on our planet and raising the overall vibrations invisibly. This is the elevation of humanity's collective consciousness, and is *the* great leap we are making now. To be living in Humanity's Spiritual Awakening does not mean that all of a sudden it's like we're living on a planetary ashram or monastery. It's just that we've awakened to our Higher Self's Presence being the more dominant force we listen to, which is aligned with Source energy and vital life force juices, rather than our ego-mind at the most basic personality and survival level, which has been what the masses have done to this point. The additional aspect here is that when we choose based on a desire that seems to whip up all of these supportive energies, events, occurrences—synchronicities or seeming coincidences that come together to make this act or choice more effortless—it is because we are doing something that causes alignment with our eternal being, or part of possibly our purpose to be here. This would naturally be something of a higher vibratory nature; selfish pursuits that are going to hurt others are getting flushed out within this new paradigm as it is increasingly ushered in.

And what if part, if not all, of our purpose was to be so full of joy that we inspire others?

What if choosing to be that in alignment with who we really are is what causes all to come into alignment around us?

What if living from choosing what is going to *not* shut us down to life, but to bring forth the energies that flush more life force juice throughout our systems, is an act of awakening?

Once we yield to this more subtle part of ourselves, increasingly we stop the cycle of all the forcing to make things happen: the controlling of as many external conditions as possible to ensure whatever we're wanting to have happen does, the need to incessantly figure out how to do it, and the remaining myriad of efforting, forcing, and controlling that the ego-mind, and still the collective deem necessary.

What if it were simply creating ourselves to be the frequency or vibration—meaning the collection of thoughts, feelings, emotions, and consciousness—that is in alignment, and from this alignment all receptivity flows?

What if we're not meant to go it alone, and feel burdened and heavy with all that life forces us to deal with?

But instead of listening to the ego-mind's small perspective that is so based in keeping one's self safe, we move more into the Observing Self, who is less concerned with remaining safe and comfortable, and more magnetized toward courageously choosing what causes us to expand and feel most alive?

What if settling wasn't the name of the game, or being and doing what most others are being and doing was no longer the game?

In making use of the meaning of Ananda's name in Sanskrit, *bliss*, is it possible to learn from Ananda's example and name and allow ourselves to be in bliss?

It is in fact by choosing this bliss over and over again that we can then activate our awakened life force. The Awakening doesn't happen first; we actually first have to choose it.

And in this choosing of it—like Ananda's desire to be a part of the council that collected all of Buddha's teachings so sacred to Ananda, as Ananda was the one who had heard them the most—and then taking inspired action based on our desire and choosing something we want—like Ananda increasing his time to meditate and diligence—that this desire and choice leads us to the guidance of what the inspired action is to take, *and we then choose it*. We don't force a council to convene nor do we force enlightenment.

So what if it's not about figuring it out *first*, and then taking action, because that is more of the Newtonian physics of the old paradigm, where things line up in that concrete, sequential, predictable, linear way?

Instead it is to learn to Observe what makes one feel blissful, choose more of that, and wait, allowing the subtle energy forces to gather momentum. As we continue to choose and stay in our bliss, we are guided through our intuitive knowing and synchronicities then show up, both showing us our next step, done within these inspired qualities or energetics. This naturally will be in alignment, and when in alignment, there is more allowing of the natural forces to continue to flow, rather than being out of alignment and having to then force, control, manipulate, push, and persuade.

Then this alignment activates all the supportive, co-creative forces within and around us as collaborators in life, this sacred divine energy flowing throughout all animate life. This choice further activates more clear energy, claiming to the universe what we desire, and so thus the increase in supportive consciousness flows toward us and our desired outcome.

When Ananda reached a peak of efforting, he let go, and there was his desired outcome. If it sounds too good to be true, that's your ego-mind throwing up its game, to keep this level of blissful living just out of your reach. Perhaps, as all of life, the existence and functionality of ego-mind are threatened if we were to live our lives in such a way that doesn't require the ego-mind so much.

If we've made the ego-mind serviceable to our overall system's needs with our Higher Self in command, isn't that then disciplining the ego-mind?

A little child may not like discipline at first, but still at some point acknowledges that the discipline is coming from a caring, loving parent. So it's okay, too, to be aware of the ego-mind's resistance and talk to it as if a little child in fear and acting out based on this fear.

But to choose more ease for one's Self and life anyway?

This in fact, I have seen, creates a more robust co-collaborative effort on behalf of the Source energies, or subtle energies, or the Universe or however you construe it, to respond with even more aligned synchronicities, perhaps in response to our continued choice for living in more alignment.

This letting go is a challenge at times to allow, but again, mostly only at first, as we cut new teeth, or rip new muscles. It gets easier as we develop more musculature, as in doing bicep curls at the gym; we have to increase the weight lifted once our muscles have been conditioned to that new weight. The more ego-mind we still have in place, the more we're going to be engaged in intellectual questioning, philosophical musings, and analytical exploration—feeling like we have to just figure it out with this process. Thus, the more we're going to keep this process and these energies at bay because we're not able to be witnesses at the lightness and subtleness where and how they exist from all the ego-mind's noise. It just simply blocks out the ability to Observe the more subtle, which is the entry point to this other world of activated life force and awakened, co-creative lives. Instead, we stay locked in, with our ego-mind doing what it does so well—maintaining the status quo.

How does that song go?

"The first cut is the deepest. . ."

So maybe it's all the crises we see and the suffering so many are engaged in because they haven't proactively chosen to rise above the ego-mind. And these crises are giving us the openings to reach out to this more significant or meaningful energy in the midst of our suffering or crisis. This becomes the way we get a hint of the subtle energies and this co-creative life force.

And if the nature of our times is in fact to do exactly that, and we're not choosing to, then this is also a momentum of its own. And so more suffering ensues, until it seems like we align with the nature of our times—our spiritual awakening collectively and, if we haven't yet, individually. Well that doesn't seem so logical, especially for the part of us that is supposed to contain the logic!

Who made up this game, anyway?

It seems that the laws and sense of humor of this universe frequently run counter-intuitively. Which again makes the shift into this multi-dimensional, or metaphysical, or life with connection to the subtle energies and working with the subtle energies to then infuse physical life in a intended, desired way, more hidden and also more significant. This is not the land of instant gratification, which is what I have seen trip up so many. There is this expectation of the same types of logic and laws in the way our ego-mind reasons projected onto the universal laws and the way life really works, the way energy actually naturally flows, the way cause and effect actually work, the way duality actually functions to create polarity. There is so much more to just learning to discipline our wild ego-mind's demands and monkey mind's noise and mayhem. So much becomes accessible and as it becomes increasingly so, the Observer is activated within us and the ego-mind has been put in its rightful place.

The more we've worked with our ego-mind and have cultivated the ability to detach from our thoughts, the less seriously we take ourselves and our thoughts. This allows for more room to play, more buoyant energy to explore new things. And it is with this light-hearted tone of an adventurer that we can approach this alignment process of allowing, rather than needing to intellectually or analytically understand each step. We don't have to figure it out or have an action plan. Its full meaning prior to taking any steps toward the desired new avenue in life that brings us more joy and will replace where we've played it safe.

The fifth chakra, again, is central to all of this, as the center containing choice, courage, and creativity. Each chakra has an element. The first is earth, second is water, third is fire, and fourth is air. It is only at the start of the fifth chakra that the elements become more ethereal, as we move into the more spiritual chakras. The fifth chakra's element is ether. When I learned this in my yoga teacher training in India, it really impressed upon me the nuanced differences between the Chinese culture's understanding of vital life force energy, or chi, and the Hindu yogic culture's understanding of vital life force energy, or prana. It seems like the Hindu yogic wisdom has more subtle levels of consciousness identified than the Chinese, due to the difference in their elements and a vast amount of other differences that deserves its own book.

The fifth chakra also has the seat of energy of upward-moving air. Each chakra has a certain quality of energy to it, also referred to as its *seat*. So within the fifth chakra, having a seat of upward-moving air shows up as choices courageously made to create our life following our bliss. There is then further opening and spinning perfectly at the fifth chakra, the vital life force energy, which brings us into further alignment with the Source and Higher Self energy that is connected through the crown chakra. An open chakra system with both its manifesting current, energy flowing down from the crown chakra to the root chakra, and its liberating current, from root chakra up to the crown, is able to flow freely and has this upward-air element activated at the fifth chakra. Our system is able to have more ease with continuing this upward surge of air—or current or direction—

to connect with Source and Higher Self at the crown chakra, the more our fifth chakra is open. Thus the more we choose to courageously create the life we desire, following our bliss, the more attunement and alignment result.

This may seem counterintuitive.

Shouldn't we be able to align more with Source and feel more of that sacred energy and feel more blissful once we have the thing we desire to create in our lives?

Well, if our world was in fact ordered with the physical as the most lasting and important, then yes, it would. But we do in fact live in a world where everything is energy and then becomes physical, based on the energetics of it. In fact, this is part of what seems to be one of the most crucial turning points of this entire gig—human beings and our choices, a.k.a. free will, which resides at the fifth chakra. So yes, not only are our free will choices integral, but our activation of the co-creative subtle forces seem to then step up the game to match our energies once we've made conscious choices for our expansion that result in our increased bliss, joy, and vitality. But it is only when coupled with this energy of following our bliss—able to be experienced because we are choosing something that honors our unique contributions with who we are, or our genius that contributes to the greater whole, or what makes us really feel on and fulfilled and naturally successful at doing this—that the *pop* can happen, and we are in alignment. Finally, in using these blissful energies as our guidance for when to choose and take inspired action, we are thus engaged in the process of the creativity inherent to the fifth chakras and our human systems, to live our lives from this bliss, or ananda. And it is this bliss that activates the principle of energy's potential seed of consciousness to come to fruition. It is the act of co-creation. But we have to choose it first—or it may choose us! — before the external conditions can change around to physically show up the way we desire them to be. And after we choose it, we need to keep choosing it and then allow for the co-creative guidance to come in now through the wisdom of our Higher Self or the Universe or divinity, however we construe it. Once we receive the guidance, we take the inspired action based on the sense of being in alignment, and feel the Yes! energy caused by this action.

Really, there is a certain reliability and logic to it. Based on the universal law of magnetics, or Law of Attraction, if we're putting forth high, light, excitement and enthusiasm over something that is inherently natural to our being, such as creating inspiring tapestries with sacred symbols for others to own and hang in their homes, meditation rooms or centers, then the law of magnetics, or the LOA, assists in bringing more of this *on*, or awakened, or activated type of energy to us, through continued opportunities. We are awakened, with the universe as our co-creator. This type of dynamic has a lot more pulling power, and a lot more of the universe's, or Source's, charmed qualities to it, than if we're just settling and relatively closed down to our mundane job that provides food, shelter, and clothing that we must do for ourselves and our families. The activation and awakened forces of our mind-body-spirit system just aren't there, creating on our behalf, and instead we're left to basically create from a dulled-down existence through the mind, and a dulled-down version of the law of magnetics, or LOA.

Chapter Seven

Satyagraha: Love or Soul Force

> *Truth (satya) implies love, and firmness (agraha) engenders and therefore serves as a synonym for force. I thus began to call the Indian movement Satyagraha, that is to say, the Force which is born of Truth and Love or nonviolence, and gave up the use of the phrase "passive resistance" in connection with it, so much so that even in English writing we often avoided it and used instead the word satyagraha.*
>
> ~ Mahatma Gandhi

> *I have also called it (satyagraha) love-force or soul-force.*
>
> ~ Mahatma Gandhi

Love is the motivation for writing this book: love for humanity, love for our planet and its beauty, its support, and its offerings. Obviously I mean that higher vibration of love and not the sticky-sweet romantic kind from the movies. It is the vibration of the essence of all love that I mean.

So what if this essence of love is a forceful love, a vigorous, dynamic force, and not a controlling and domineering force?

This force has fertility and creativity naturally built into it. And the quality has a sort of effervescence to it, like refrigerated kombucha tea or ginger ale.

From Wikipedia:

> **Satyagraha** (Sanskrit: मरूऋग्वरूद्गरूश्ररू *satyāgraha*) is the idea of nonviolent resistance (fighting with peace) started by Mahatma Gandhi. Gandhi used satyagraha in the Indian independence movement and also during his earlier struggle in South Africa. Satyagraha helped shape Nelson Mandela's struggle in South Africa under apartheid, Martin Luther King, Jr.'s campaigns during the civil rights movement in the United States, and many other similar movements. Someone who practices satyagraha is a *satyagrahi*.

Therefore is it possible that there is a love force or a soul force behind it all, behind this vital life force, or prana, or chi?

I know that in my studies of chi gong and Taoist tonic herbalism, chi is very much presented as a neutral force, a non-spiritualized concept.

But is this what is meant by the universal life force, with "universal" replaced by "love"?

What is the most universal energy or permeating substance that all human life hungers for, and that hurts humans most, and not having it, humans resort to the most inane acts?

Is this what causes all suffering?

If someone is hungry and requires bread, is it not an act of love when another human sees the hungry one's need and provides the bread?

So while we could say it is the bread — or the lack of food — causing the suffering, in fact if this person had love flowing through his own being, he'd be sure to have loved himself enough to do what it takes to take better care of himself.

It's a risky thing that I just said. It sounds cold and callous (and even some politicos would say Republican, if American). But after twenty years of having thousands of clients show their systems to me, what calms a system the most is this sense of being safe.

What makes a human feel safe?

That they're warm?

Sure.

But doesn't love warm?

That they're well fed.

Well, what feeds?

Love.

What do we survive on in the first years of our lives?

Our mother's milk, right?

And within that act of breastfeeding — or a mother making sure her baby is fed when the baby is crying — isn't that an act of love?

So, in fact, isn't it the love that we're seeking that then shows up as food, shelter, and clothing?

And what about people who have their basic needs covered?

What are they then looking for?

Money?

How often have we each heard the phrase, "Money can't buy love"?

And by now, in our post-modernized, globalized society, is an advanced and comfortable part of the population, at least the majority reading this book, who can see the dissatisfaction of the most wealthy, the extremely wealthy, the wealthy, and the moderately wealthy. It's not money that they're seeking as much as feelings of love and approval and safety through the money or beyond the money.

So is it accurate to say that when I have clients on my table, and I'm helping rewire their systems' flow of life force, that it is in fact love force?

Love heals all. That's one common euphemism.

We hear, "Love conquers all."

And then we hear, "Love is at the root of it all."

When I drink fresh, live kombucha, or I when I drove home when living in Asia on my scooter after just having picked up freshly made organic yogurt, I can feel the aliveness of the healthy bacteria almost singing. It's like I've got a group of kindergarteners with me, who are excited to play and climb trees, not in a hyperactive way, but with a full-on excitement for life and *go* way. In fact, I was just talking with a client today about how the good bacteria that we take to support the health of our gut — so central to our systemic health and vitality — have an energetic quality to them that is more alive and speaks to me in a way that few other inanimate objects do. For me, this proves it's life force or perhaps love force. And in the love force is the ability to assist us in staying strong and healthy. Many cultures say that the health of the immune system resides in the gut, due to these friendly bacteria.

I remember teaching my global psychology class to high school students as an elective the year before I began teaching advanced-placement psychology from the standardized, university-level text used in most psychology introductory courses. I designed this global psychology class to be a merger of Buddhism's science of mind and the West's psychology. I used the Dalai Lama's texts, which were actual transcripts from his bi-annual summits with scientists, including psychologists from the West, as the texts supporting the "science of mind" components of the course. My students and I were in a discussion about whether the basic human tendencies were inherently good or evil.

The Dalai Lama's answer to this is, paraphrased: "Well, human beings throughout millennia have basically been constructive, working together to keep communities functioning. If you grew rice and I made pots, then we would each trade so that we could each have cooked rice to support our families. If we were inherently evil, then we would have destructed our existence a long time ago. The fact that we continue to predominantly work constructively together is a testament to the inherent goodness of humans."

I so cherished—and still do—this explanation. It says and implies so much, with saying so little. This is something I find the Chinese tend to master, by the way.

So is it possible to extrapolate from the Dalai Lama's explanation and say that anything that is constructively working toward building or constructing life is essentially a force of love?

If we look at a tree, its branches grow up and out. The same is true for flowers and humans. We don't grow smaller; we expand.

That is the inherent nature of our life force and of energy itself. All life wants to expand.

So if this is the inherent nature of the vital life force pulsing through us, and its basic nature is to support us constructively to build and create our lives, is it then appropriate to say it is an act of love to expand and grow beyond what we has been previously?

I also know that to take clients from depression to enjoyment and fulfillment with their lives, I am seeing a life force come alive. And within that clearing out of what typically feels thick and gray, like a coating over them as if suppressing their aliveness, they come alive, and it's like they've become a fountain, able to spout life force, or love force. Their zeal for life is restored, and they go about creating a life they feel is worth living, and creating and allowing themselves to create what they actually desire. Once this force is opened, and in particular the fifth chakra, the aspects of choosing, creating, and courage are awakened to a fully functional level.

Isn't there a certain amount of love involved, in both the love for Self and the love for life, that is being restored?

One of my male clients is professionally employed, the father of two young girls, and happily married to a woman who is a nurse practitioner. They both support the family's needs, although more of the financial burden tends to fall on my client, as his wife works only part time in order to be home with their girls and not use daycare. His job helps others who are handicapped use computers, by educating them about how to use the technology his company developed. It's a fulfilling job, but he's bored. He feels stuck and afraid to make any other choices. He has felt this way increasingly over the past four years. And so he ended up anxious and depressed. He was suppressing his life force energy that wanted to and wants to express itself in a new way that raised him above his old, safe, status-quo existence. In other words, at his system's Higher Self's level, he wanted to expand. And this expansion involved new challenges, like creating a food truck based on his talented cooking abilities and offering healthy gourmet pizzas. He has been learning to meditate and has increasingly been cultivating mindfulness as a result. He now notices when his mind goes into fear and anxiety and depression and is able to allow those thoughts to pass without the ensuing bodily biochemical reaction it once was locked into. He has also begun to be more open to the splendor of life, looking up more often and seeing more birds, while also noticing the little things once overlooked by a busy, turned off, cynical ego-mind just getting by due to the settling his awakened consciousness is now able to notice. With the ongoing support of my weekly group call, he is slowly finding his ability to dream of all that he wants to create is awakened, revealing a fifth chakra that is in the process of getting cleared and the creativity within it coming alive.

That fifth chakra is an intensely intriguing one for me, especially in these times. With all three aspects—courage, creativity, and choice—located within this chakra, and all three contributing to creating and choosing a life of alignment, again this seems like the chakra is key to freeing us up for more tangible expression in daily life. Remembering that this creativity is not the arts-and-crafts kind, but the kind that is behind our choices that create our lives, then our creativity to do so requires varying degrees of courage in order to choose to expand our lives beyond the level of settling or comfort or status quo and into something that is genuinely blissful. That, again, is when our systems most thrive.

Coming back to the vital life force energy itself, as a personal trainer and vegetarian for more than twenty-five years and after living in Asia for ten years exploring theories and practices for longevity, I know that longevity typically involves two things. One is tonic herbalism. Two is an exercise practice that involves interacting with, moving, and cultivating subtle energy. These subtle energies are what the good bacteria feel like: really happy. It is this awakened, alive force and zest for life that clients come to me to have restored. I am talking about clients from around the world and of all ages, from their teens up to their nineties. Everyone is hungry for that life force.

Another thing I learned in my research on longevity and tonic herbalism, and my training in both chi gong and yoga, is that we are made to be fountains sprouting our life force—and if we are not, then something within us is causing an energy drain. That is something *within us*, *not* something outside of us. The point is that people, having low levels of vitality, are drained. And they're drained because they're not living a life that causes them to feel activated, energized, awakened, and alive. There is an understanding in these fields that if one does not have a sex drive, that is an indicator of the foundational levels of energy not being supported; something is amiss within the *jing*, or the primal life force, and also the chi, the daily life energy supply, or even the *shen*, the heart's energy coupled with the spirit's energy. All three of these components are the core to traditional Chinese medicine's tonic herbalism, otherwise known as the three treasures.

This life force in the energy medicine—my first certification of the five different modalities I learned—is the energy medicine that I eventually created.

The energy medicine I chose to make mine that most encompasses what I do is Vibrational UPgrade energy medicine.

Why?

Due to those erroneous beliefs that we take on at the unconscious and subconscious levels due to our conditions upon birth and formative years and hence our conditioning, we have beliefs that are not from love at its source. And as we've been consistently examining, these erroneous beliefs or traumas stop energy and congeal into a block, which is entangled energy. Reviewing for a moment here, this then causes specific chakras—depending on the belief that correlates to a certain chakra, as each chakra covers a domain of life—to shut down and no longer turn this life force, or chi, or prana. Or perhaps even love force or satyagraha is stopped from being allowed to flow in that area of the body and is the domain of life the chakra is connected to, depending on the belief structure's contents.

If it's about survival and foundational support—food, shelter, clothing, feeling wanted—then it's the root, right?

The idea and intent behind my Vibrational UPgrade energy medicine is to allow the mind-body-spirit system to exist as it was intended to be. One that is vibrantly alive, singing with joy and elation, with our spirits firmly grounded in our bodies. One in which we're no longer engaged in check-out mechanisms and just getting by because our lives, as we've created them thus far, are simply not enjoyable enough. These distractions include shopping, web surfing, Internet porn, eating, drinking, watching TV or YouTube videos, group sports, or whatever is our means of checking out of our lives.

This calls us to be an embodied presence in our bodies, behind our eyes and taking command over our lives with an awakened, empowered, activated Presence that is consciously choosing certain things and consciously *not* choosing other things. This is creating our lives as we desire them to be, rather than merely accepting or settling for the lives everyone around us is living. In the past there was no real choice, it was just life as we knew it and have known it. As we lighten up from the density that the unconscious and subconscious outdated beliefs function as, and as we clear our mind-body-spirit systems of these blocks, our life force, or prana, can freely flow throughout the chakra column, affecting every area of our lives. It's all interrelated. Our mind's unconscious beliefs reside in whatever chakra covers the domain of life where the block resides. The blocks are the erroneous beliefs that shut our systems down — chakra, body, mind, and life — rather than flow life force energy throughout it. The unconsciousness resides throughout the body, within the chakras, which are the intersections of the mind, body, and spirit. The subconscious beliefs that function as blocks could be thought to be in our minds, more specifically the back part of our brain, at the occipital lobe. This is our most reptilian and reactive wiring, but it still influences the relevant chakras, so it still shuts the flow of vital life force energy to that part of life and body the belief and chakra are related to.

Therefore, no matter the tool used from within my various trainings and practices, it is all geared toward assisting clients' mind-body-spirit systems to have an overall Vibrational UPgrade. As we clear out the blocks, there's more vital life force flowing throughout their systems. As there's more vital life force flowing throughout their systems, then that's a higher vibration, one that is closer to that elusive term, *enlightenment*. All food, thoughts, practices, habits, feelings, clothing, and choices — everything in life has a frequency or vibration to it. Love is the highest vibration; fear is the lowest. As we go about our lives making choices, we're either contributing to our vibration, raising to a higher, lighter state, or we're weighing ourselves down at a more stagnant, fear-based state. It depends on where our overall system's habitual set point has been building its momentum, vibrationally, on a daily basis.

When all of the chakras are opened because someone has done the clearing out of the foundational energy patterns, this accomplishes the mining and self-exploration that targets the parts of their lives that seem the most stuck. This is because I'm going in and seeing which chakras are the most stuck, while also knowing the reason the client has come to me, and getting them unstuck. Although frequently, the reason people think they're coming to me is not what ultimately is the cause, nor the result, of our working together. And the vital life force then becomes unstuck throughout their entire system, so they are now flowing bubbling, effervescent life force throughout their systems.

Another dynamic that people often come to me with is when their observable behavior differs from what they *say* they want. Sometimes they've been working toward it for years, *but* their behavior indicates that they're in fact *not* working for it or going for it, meaning they're engaged in self-sabotage. But they don't even see it because they're not detached enough, able to Observe their own behaviors' incongruities with what they're saying they want. So it does *not* seem from their observable behavior that they in fact do want this thing, like a new job, since they're not sending out any new resumes and instead during their free time watch Netflix. We therefore end up clearing out the unconsciousness around the chakra relevant to procrastination, and the specific beliefs within that domain of life they're sabotaging themselves in. For example, this could be earning money in a way that is meaningful and fulfilling to them and engages them, rather than accepting with sardonic sarcasm that this is all that is available to them and they have to settle for this way of earning income, likely due to the amount of people who are depending on them for support. This is in fact a series of hidden beliefs stacked upon one another that keep this locked down; where they *say* they desire change, but it does *not* change.

Much of the time I have found people's conditioning very deep in not believing they can actually live the lives they desire, and create and have and be what they actually want.

It's also along the lines of the saying, "We're more afraid of our power than our weaknesses."

But frequently it's just that *so* many of us are just settling for what our lives are that the dominant paradigm still does not reflect to us that we can in fact have the lives we desire. That's only for the special few, it seems to most. This also can occur even when people are taking seemingly active steps toward this one thing they desire—target or goal, let's say—and the path to it is ridden with obstacles and difficulties and it just doesn't seem to get going, no matter how much efforting and forcing and controlling they exert. This again is symptomatic of having hidden unconsciousness around this domain of life and subconscious beliefs and blocks, and therefore requires these foundational energy patterns to be unwound.

These entangled, unconscious beliefs and where they actually exist within a person can be revealed with some self-exploration. It's even easier for me to identify almost instantly what chakra I need to work on, depending again on what domain of life clients are stuck in. You could do it yourself by going to my page with the *Chakra Attunement Audio Series* and looking through the aspects for each chakra. Over time, I've seen that for many it may be not believing that they can really have what they want, because all they see around them are people just accepting their lives as they are without really fully enjoying what they're doing. And they believe that's just the way it is. The official stats hover around 80 percent of all Americans who report being miserable at their jobs.

So the attitude of "that's just the way it is," is extremely prevalent, although is not necessarily something that is said out loud.

Instead it is usually seen in the amount of distractions they have to check out of their lives, their posture, in their levels of low energy and vitality—and in lacking that zest for life, that life force sprouting forth. It has also ended up being one of my primary focuses with my Tuesday night group clearings and activations call, because so many people present this belief.

It is the time of Awakening on our planet. Living with awakened vital life force—soul force? Love force?—is the name of the game now. We are meant to live our lives at that level of glee, joy, and fulfillment and people who tell you otherwise have their own blocks to clear!

In the most simplistic terms, Wikipedia offers a description of prana:

> **Prana** (Sanskrit: प्राण, *prāṇa*) is the Sanskrit word for "life force" or vital principle. In Hindu philosophy including yoga, Indian medicine [Ayurveda, I'm adding], and martial arts, the term refers collectively to all cosmic energies, permeating the Universe on all levels. It is the sum total of all energy that is manifest and while prana is often referred to as the "life force" or "life energy," it also includes energies present in inanimate objects. Prana is the prime mover of all activity and is energy that creates, protects, and destroys. In the literature, prana is sometimes

described as originating from the Sun and connecting the elements of the Universe.

In living beings, the universal principle of energy or force of prana, is considered responsible for the body's life, heat, health, and maintenance . . . It is analogous to chi.

Is it possible that it could be considered an act of non-violence — *ahimsa* within the yogic teachings, and taught to also be applied to the self — to allow ourselves to actually go for and have the life that is worth living, the one we dreamed of as a child, before all the seriousness of the adult responsibilities and possibly hurts from the past caused us to go into settling?

Is it possible that allowing ourselves to create a life that has everything in it that we could wish for — more the feelings and less the material, but the material possessions are included here — is an act not only of nonviolence toward ourselves, but also an act of self-love?

Is the nature of our times to not cop out and settle with the status quo, but to live an awakened, nonviolent life, as a satyagrahi?

Chapter Eight

Turiya: The Fourth State of Consciousness

Human consciousness is at a stage of evolution where the collective unconscious is primarily manifesting through the first three states of awareness: waking, sleeping, and dreaming. The fourth state, turiya, exists as a potential. Anything we know about it can never reveal its mysterious powers that create quantum shifts in our consciousness.

~ Yogi Amrit Desai, a.k.a. Gurudev

If there is an all-permeating life force at the core of all life, and it's measurable with electrical and magnetic measuring equipment, (e.g., EEG and EKG machines) and it's able to be cultivated (e.g., with meditation, tonic super-herbs, chi gong, and yoga), does this level of subtle energy, or consciousness, also contain light?

And if so, within that light does it contain information?

Many say this is all interchangeable at some level; I can feel this while working with it on behalf of my clients' systems. This energy I am working with flowing and directing into my clients' systems interacts with their chi, or *ki* (Japanese for chi, and part of the energy healing modality *reiki*). As I go about listening and guiding the energy according to my guidance and their systems' information, the energy, or ki, shows itself to have an intelligence of its own.

What does this look like?

I could have a client come in; let's call her Jo.

I ask her, "If we are living in a universe with unlimited possibilities, and now is the time to activate this, what then do you desire for yourself?"

Jo responds that she desires to have her lower back stop aching, her tinnitus to ease up, her heart to open to more receiving, and the clarity to finally see what it is she is supposed to be doing with her life. After the initial balancing of her central nervous system with her feet on the rock-salt foot lamps, we get her on the table. I begin to work at her head, with her intentions in mind. As I do this, I also listen to what her system tells me, whether it's about her mental, emotional, physical, or spiritual life, because they're all intertwined. And as I open up her system from this perspective, while working at her crown chakra, the energy medicine I've activated begins to shoot through her body.

She reacts with her legs lifting off the table, kicking and flinching, from the energy getting through, and may even report to me, "Ow! There's a tightness going on in my hip right now!"

To which I respond, "It's okay. It's just the energy breaking up the blocked, stagnant energy. It's what energy does."

Yet we were supposedly focused on her lower back, physically, right?

That was what she claimed was hurting.

However, in that surrender to my guidance—receiving information from her system and to whatever the energy sees to do—I recognize that there must be a blockage at the hip and therefore the second chakra, which then affects her lower back. With others reporting lower back pain, this could stem from the root chakra, and the energy could first go to their ankles and knees before the lower back opens up from the energy flowing to it. This movement of prana, or energy, on its own accord has occurred from day one of my working with energy medicine and hasn't stopped. The vital life force energy, or chi, has an intelligence of its own—thankfully! I am not in charge. However much work I've done to make my ego-mind serviceable and remain in a receptive stance on behalf of my clients, it is a relief to know that it's not all up to me. It is up to my ability to empty, get out of the way, and allow the energy to come through me, and prepare myself to be a strong vessel to be able to be a channel for this energy to run through me to the client. Yet ultimately, I'm not the only one making choices here.

What's also interesting, and another subtle nuance of flowing energy within a session—and more of a side note—is that the more advanced and awakened clients are, the more I can feel and see their Higher Self actively reach out and grab and direct the energy. The less clients are awakened and living from their Higher Self, the more I am left to do and direct, balanced with getting out of the way of the energy to allow it to do what it does. This is a more advanced nuance, but worth noting nonetheless, as there are different gradations I can see of how people's Higher Selves interact with the energy once they're awakened. I suppose this shows that the more awakened a person's Higher Self is, the more this inner knowing couples and dances with the energies, pranas, innate intelligence.

This is primary to learning any energy medicine technique—that our life force, or ki, has its own innate intelligence and knows what to do. In another example and building on this concept, I have had clients coming in complaining of tight hips, so I'll use the energy medicine and it flows from my hands as I work at their heads, rather than starting right off at the hips, with my hands directing energy into the hips. So when I'm at the head, the energy is still flowing down to their hips, which they've complained of being tight, because my clients report to me a variety of sensations in their lower limbs when I'm at their heads. I've also seen their legs and feet kick and jerk a bit, as the prana breaks up stagnation while I'm still at their head. So in this example of the client coming to me with the tight hips, while I'm still at her head, the client's lower back starts to have some tightness, which she remark on to me.

Chasing the pain is what this is called in the profession, in that as stagnation of energy or blocks are cleared, it opens the area around it, where the energy flows through, causing some pain in the next tight area. My client and I were relatively focusing on the hips, let's say, and yet the energy flowed to the lower back, reflected in her experiencing pain there for approximately three to five minutes before it dissipated. But what this says is that the lower back needed attention first. When the priorities that her system and the ki have are taken care of, it may then begin to flow toward the knee. So it becomes, as a practitioner, more an aspect of learning how to understand and cultivate myself and my vibration and render my ego-mind serviceable in such a way as to fluidly allow this, rather than interfere with it. Further, if clients end up with their entangled blocks of unconsciousness freed up, and they end up literally and idiomatically feeling lighter, then that seems to imply that this force has light to it—and intelligence to it, as we've just explored, as well.

We can build on that understanding now, creating a fuller appreciation here of the inherent beauty of our human design, by bringing in Gandhi's understanding of satyagraha.

If this life force energy has love at its core, then isn't that a force that wants the best for us, and for us to have all our desires met?

If it naturally is able to sense where the weakest link is in a person's mind-body-spirit system and automatically goes there first, isn't that indicative that this intelligence has love as its most basic force?

Is it anthropocentric to project this human behavior onto this life force energy?

Yet as a practitioner working with this life force in many different capacities (chi gong, yoga, meditation, energy medicine practitioner, fitness nutrition certification, and tonic herbalism background), it is impossible to deny that the various applications of this life force energy — like the ones just named — are life sustaining.

Hence, the translation into *vital life force energy*. Anything that has become an entanglement of energy I then go in and assist to unwind so clients' systems return to flowing their life force energy without stagnation, or blocks. They are then freed up in various areas of their lives, minds, and bodies.

Doesn't this imply that even when we mess something up with our thinking and thus choices and become stuck, *the sheer act of being able to get unstuck* implies that the nature of our lives, or our baseline, is health and well-being?

If the nature of our existence is based on this, doesn't it make Gandhi's discussion of satyagraha more reasonable that in fact this is also a love force, or a soul force?

Yes, we can see that it is highly likely that this light, this electromagnetic life force, quite likely has this satyagraha at its core, at a more refined level. Consciousness works in layers, and the more we do to uncover where we're unconscious, the more consciousness is revealed to us. This is huge, and it requires experiential embodiment at each level of unveiling, so that we are able to be guided by our own progressive opening, to gradually reveal more of what this life force really is doing, and what it's really about. This means learning more about both our own consciousness and the nature of consciousness.

It seems important to add a reminder here that when speaking of love being at the core, at a much more refined level to our prana, that we're not talking about the romantic love depicted in movies or country songs, but the high, piercing yet nurturing energy that contains magnetism and power and sustains all life.

Indeed, isn't life created from this force, again both literally and idiomatically?

I love looking at English idioms; English literature was my final major for my bachelors and what I taught in the classroom for twelve years, with fitness electives and AP psychology electives sprinkled in on top of this core. I have looked at our idioms in English differently since learning about subtle energy—and learning the Chinese language. It seems that these phrases are based more on the roots of English, which are connected back to our romantic-language-based cultures. These are the West's ancient societies' observations of subtle energies' affects on our bodies and lives.

This is one of the main pleasures I had while learning the Chinese language; their vast use of idioms have such a succinct way to take what is typically a full phrase in English to describe the most basic aspects of life with three characters that compose one word, which becomes understood (memorized) as an idiom, with an implied meaning. So to look at the literal meaning of the characters did not help me learn Chinese. Instead, I had to learn how the meanings were actually used. And almost always, it was applied to a wise understanding of the human being and life. Some of our most frequently used idioms in English also contain some nuggets of how our ancients in the West viewed basic life principles.

Why is this important?

Because so many are so hesitant to go beyond the science of this, to consider the animating force behind the science of it, afraid of asserting anything nonscientific or not proven, or not factual. In my first book, *What if There's Nothing Wrong?*, I traced the separation of church and science, where science was left to study the external objects of God's created Universe, and the church's domain was considered to be the internal life, which included the supernatural. This left no science in the West examining the internal world of the human, or the unseen aspects of our physically manifest world.

It is only recently that tools to pick up the more subtle, less crude, or less gross physical objects have begun to be developed, and that's basically since globalization and access to the East has increased. Meanwhile, the East accesses the West's materialized lifestyle. In the West, after the first decade of last century, quantum physics began to focus on the more subtle aspects of life based on an unintended result of an experiment, where the Observer effect was first witnessed in an experiment. But it has taken more than a century for the more orthodox halls of science to allow for this type of research. What has come to be known as the new science has basically been the field merging the study of the subtle with the scientific method. And new science is still considered the bad stepchild of real science. Much of this appears to be due to where the funding comes from to support science.

So now we've had some tools, equipment, and machines to measure the chi, or the prana, and thus there has been a crack in the walls of science to focus only on the physically tangible. Or, at least, in accordance with how it was used to dualistically construe the physical from the internal. I consider chi to be more physical than other levels of consciousness, for example the prana I'm working with when it runs through the throat chakra, whose element is ether. There are also more tools to measure chi that have been created in the East. These help us to see from a different cultural perspective, steeped in the cultural milieu that the East is, both how to apply these measurements of a vital life force energy for our benefit, and innately designing tools from a more subtle perspective to begin with, due the nature of living in the Eastern hemisphere.

In the West there has been that historical split between church and science, and those in the West are immersed in this, without perhaps being fully conscious of all that this then creates. A bias toward the physical, and a bias toward measurement, a bias toward proof, and a distrust of anything that has not been proven are a few of the more impactful beliefs.

But it seems that this book is not being written for those still wrangling within themselves over allowing the nonphysical more presence in their lives, as my first book was geared. During these times of Humanity's Spiritual Awakening, those who have already awakened are looking for how to further this awakening in a meaningful way that impacts their everyday lives. This could mean not working at a job that drains them of all spirit due to their complete lack of interest in what they're doing forty-plus hours a week, and replacing that with work that supports them in following their bliss.

This awakening time seems to be supporting us in following our bliss and creating our lives based on bliss. Some would even say it's nonnegotiable, a conspiracy of sorts. This act of creation, of recognizing that we are creating our lives through our choices, coupled with some other force assisting us in this co-creation, seems to be a major aspect emerging from these new times. Involved in this is our beginning to slow down enough to Observe, or become conscious of, where we are in fact creating our lives through our choices, but before we may not have even realized we had in fact made a choice for this, and not *that*, and to do *this*, but not *that*.

Part of this is occurring as we gradually replace remaining in that dualistic approach begun in the West centuries ago of inside versus outside. And ensuingly, that which is observable as what's on the outside and what is on the inside isn't really information that we're meant to have. Our doctors, priests, and rabbis have historically occupied this domain, along with psychotherapists, for some. Our focus here has been on the physically tangible, because that's what's more important and has more power. Doubting the relevance and importance of the invisible — and even fearing it — we in the West have historically been shunned away from examining our internal worlds of thoughts, feelings, emotions, energy, or consciousness. This is a direct contrast to what has been created and cultivated in the East.

This outdated paradigm that also orients its citizens toward looking for something or someone outside of them as the source that controls the conditions (e.g., the economy), and then blaming the external conditions only. Another paradox tightly—and quite subtly—interwoven in here is that this does not typically yield citizens slowed down enough to Observe the intricacies within their beliefs, as they're in the process of making the choices that then end up as the lives they're living. We remain on the survival level of life, in accordance with the physical and in reaction to what the five physical senses present us with, in a cultural milieu that supports results on the physically tangible plane—productivity, commodification, monetization, and measurable results. Tangible tokens of success create more focus on the physical plane of care, payment, insurance, upkeep, and all the rest to maintain all the physically produced objects considered to be the symbols of success. So that, too, keeps people on a certain type of hamster wheel, locked into and onto the physical plane.

If we are attuned to the outward manifestations, and not the internal processes of our thoughts, feelings, emotions, and bodily cues, then we won't be attuned to notice—or Observe—where we are in fact making choices. We choose what routes to take to work, what food to eat, what jobs to get, what standard of living we desire, what type of lifestyle we desire (i.e., live to work or work to live), what kind of work culture to exist within, what stores we shop in, what types of people we typically associate and don't associate with, and what types of social events we typically consider going to. And what ones totally fall off of our radar and on and on to every minute detail. We are the ones choosing all of it. Upon first hearing this, it does require much consideration and is part of quite a gradual shift, of embodied, experiential unveiling of how this does in fact occur. Increasingly this is what I teach and coach my clients and students on day in and day out. Gradually, after unwinding enough layers of unconsciousness and bringing more consciousness to light—quite literally, as you can see by this point—this then becomes a life-long embracing of learning how to be the co-creator of harmony, well-being, and bliss. And it is what this book is aimed at, and where we are going next, in these upcoming years, as we enter further into Humanity's Spiritual Awakening.

So in a paradigm such as the one we're living within here in the West, where we're geared toward looking at the physical world, focusing on productivity follows suit. So this orientation toward the inside of us (e.g., energy levels, food cravings, and thoughts) isn't a natural part of a citizen living within this paradigm. For further appreciation of this, let's contrast this with life in an Eastern country. Most have a holistic medical system — even if they have taken on Western medicine in full as well — that includes as valuable information within reporting the symptomology consideration of stress levels, emotions of recent days preceding a visit to the doctor, and typical foods consumed. The entire backdrop of the Western meta-paradigm of all aspects of our society is not geared toward the holistic, nor looking beyond the physically tangible. These are related and it is cyclical.

This participation we each have in the creation of our lives, communities, societies, industries, paradigm, and meta-paradigm is not seen at the more subtle levels. These more subtle levels are where our own unconscious and subconscious beliefs are, causing us to allow for only this one choice that we've always made because that's what everyone else is doing. Or because we believe that's how it's always been done, or because we are simply following along without even realizing that we are following along. We're making a choice, let's say, to marry and have kids, buy a home, and have a job that pays for this mortgage, kids' tuitions, clothing, and food. This could be viewed in the context of other possible choices, say instead living as an expat, maybe married, maybe not, maybe in a tiny house debt-free rather than a standard American home with the average size of 2,500 square feet, or on some beach or in some remote village in a different country that may have a lower standard of living, a slower pace, and therefore a different emphasis on what we do day in and day out. Choices, choices, choices. Life is in fact a buffet! We are meant to be living a joyous existence, not a shutdown one where we've settled.

My client, Alex, is an environmental scientist focused on global warming. Or he was when we began working together approximately eighteen months ago. Alex is in his mid-sixties. He has been working from home for twenty years. When he reached out to me, he had heard me on an interview, liked what he heard and how he felt after I provided an experiential process to lighten up the audience, raising the vibrations by clearing out subconscious and unconscious blocks. He bought my *Chakra Attunement Audio Series*, and then reached out to work with me one-on-one because he noticed the more tangible results he was getting from listening again and again to the clearings on those MP3s for each chakra. One that excited him a lot was that he was feeling lighter and happier. I came to learn later why this was so important to him.

We began working together, and he wasn't very specific about what he desired. He didn't really know, in fact, which is an aspect of a weak fifth chakra. The throat-neck chakra is the chakra of choice and creativity, which is applied to our lives through our choices we make that do in fact create our lives. And it's interesting to note and quite informative to consider that the sense of strangulation — being restricted or limited — is a sensation held at the neck. Alex just knew that he liked how he was feeling from being exposed to my work and wanted to feel that way more. In that first one-on-one session, he was startled by what my intuition picked up within him and that I was able to articulate what I saw, as it named key, foundational, life-long challenges of his—and it earned me the Hawkeyes nickname. As we went on, with my continuing to treat him with weekly one-one-one sessions from a distance—I live in Florida, he lives in Canada—some of the other foundational energy patterns I told him I saw in his chakras continued to bring to life, or bring to his conscious mind, habits and patterns and feelings of which he'd been unconscious. This provided tremendous relief and awakening in him.

One of the main aspects I saw was that his fifth chakra was severely shut down, and it was connected to a few other chakras that were also shut down due to two different foundational energy patterns that had been wired into him during his developmental years. One was that he was used to feeling burdened with having to prove himself because his dad didn't encourage him to believe in himself, especially his intellect, calling Alex "stupid." Another was that he was used to being treated badly and not being able to say anything about it.

He grew up feeling like he needed to prove his dad wrong. After an initial response of poor grades to his father's discouragement over Alex's intellectual capacities, Alex then got encouragement one year from a special high school teacher, and off he was on the track to being a scientist. He is quite successful in his field. His first marriage failed because he didn't speak up for himself much, instead remaining quietly burdened with the charge of being the responsible one in his marriage, while his ex-wife did whatever she felt like, including cheating on him at the end.

His job was not in a field that people were really responsive to twenty years ago. He chose a field to apply himself when very few people at the time were at all concerned about global warming. Furthermore, he then went into an area of global warming in which he wrote progressive assessments for clients who asked to understand the environmental impact on global warming, but these aren't required by the government, so the compliance or follow-through on his suggestions was weak. Over time, this ultimately disheartened him, quite literally. With the work he chose to ultimately specialize in, he was speaking to folks who were only partially listening because they weren't overly concerned about implementing his suggestions.

Do you see the pattern, or the similarities?

Alex was unheard in his work, while working on something that was hugely important to him—and us all. When we first started working together and he would talk about his work, he was fed up, angry, and righteously indignant over the entire situation, including the average citizen's lack of concern about global warming. He was that discouraged. Alex is a gentle, soft, kind man. Global warming is obviously a huge issue; only just recently have we seen people making more choices based on wanting to respond proactively to this threat. Certainly not twenty years ago! So after some time had passed and he had quite a few sessions under his belt, so to speak, I chose to intermittently redirect his focus to see that people were increasingly concerned and there were behavioral changes, including economic ones, to help alleviate the strain on the Earth. But I didn't do too much of that, only at choice moments when I saw that it would land, and he would hear it. So I waited, and kept delivering clearings and upgrades to his chakras and system. Ultimately, what really seemed to assuage him was the relief from the shifts he was embodying at increasing levels from these clearings and upgrades within his system. He felt these changes mentally, emotionally, physically, and spiritually. As he has gotten lighter, he has become less willing to make it his burden and responsibility to solve global warming.

Alex gradually became more conscious, or aware, as it was revealed to him through our sessions how his choices for both his marriage and his work were unconsciously connected to his childhood. He felt he was not heard growing up and was discouraged to become anything worthwhile, so there was an overall lack of receptivity to him, his desires, and views. I continued to work at unwinding the foundational energy patterns entangled up in three main chakras, with secondary impacts distributed throughout his entire system. This can illuminate an example of the secondary impacts, which were that his heart chakra was relatively closed down because he wasn't feeling particularly connected to anyone from working alone. This was also affected by the level of receptivity for his assessments and therefore he ended up even more so, feeling less open and receptive to folks in general. And then we worked on his deeply personal hurt from the betrayal in his marriage. After working through these, we got to even older effects, with some seemingly linked to this one specific past life overall — it seemed like his last one — where he was speaking up for the resistance, as one of the leaders in a concentration camp, and was unheard. There was much trauma locked up in this event and this took quite an intensive focus by me to cleanly unwind all of the effects out of his chakras and system.

Over time, I delivered distant energy medicine session to his chakras — as we're trained to do in reiki from a symbol we're attuned to that opens up the ethereal gate, so to speak, and other modalities train in concepts along this line, as well — and I would then send him the detailed notes after each session and we'd talk about them the next session. He gradually began to see where he was unconscious about behaviors that to him had felt like his personality. But he was able to see and feel and experience the new behaviors emerging — some quite surprised him and this gave me glee to observe! — as he saw himself speaking up more for himself, desiring to go out and connect with more folks, feeling lighter and less burdened, feeling more confident and energized, and detaching from his need to be heard with the work he was doing. He experienced this contrast of these new behaviors from new choices now made available to him because conscious awareness replaced what had once been no awareness that he had actually made those choices. Yet these choices, and more importantly, that in fact there were other possibilities, remained under his conscious radar due to what he had subconsciously and unconsciously been geared—limited—toward choosing.

As Alex and I increasingly cleared out that fifth chakra, he chose to go down to part-time work about a year and a half into our working together. He had been feeling like he wanted to honor these newfound feelings of lightness and joy after what has felt like decades of depression. In fact, he had been on antidepressants and had taken himself off them before we began working together. Alex increasingly saw what else was possible for him to choose now that his unconscious energetic blocks were unblocked and the chakras opened and more life force flowing through them and thus his overall system (mind-body-spirit). This freed up the consciousness for awareness in these areas of his life. And this has allowed him to make different choices than before, when he felt locked in with not many options or choices available. Ultimately, Alex is working toward retiring in three months, which will be two years after we first began working together. He has set himself free!

I'm sorry for the repetition, but having lived in contrast to this system for over a decade while in Asia, the West's emphasis on the physically tangible and not the subtle, and the taking-care-of-business approach to living life in the post-modernized, globalized world of today—and let's face it, more so in the non-siesta-taking United States— combine together to create a culture that prioritizes (many say glorifies) the physically manifest over the more subtle in life. It is the exact opposite in the East. And now in the West there is a growing number of awakened folks like you who are realizing that what shows up on the outside is a result of what is on the inside.

However, if people perceive that they're locked into a life of productivity and measured outcomes that others can see and point to as achievements—a game of the ego-mind— then it seems that, within this current vibrational backdrop to our greatest evolutionary leap in humanity, they're likely feeling the pressure to perpetuate this cultural meta-paradigm's hamster wheel. It's as if there's a peaking of the old before it can dissipate, in a way. Some folks need it get worse before it gets better, so it seems. They're living with increasing tightness possibly, and without awareness of other choices being possible, both in general and personally for themselves. This leaves little to no space or consideration for Observing their thoughts.

You see it clearer now, yes?

Meditating or learning to be attuned to looking within is too subtle for the lifestyle they're living within because their focus hasn't been attenuated internally. It seems, too, that the creations made from this type of constriction don't seem to be able to gain as much ground anymore, as this outdated meta-paradigm loses its firm hold on the collective.

The fertile yields of this internal focus aren't easily communicated, nor readily understood until they're experienced. In order to get to the point of experiencing them, we have to be slowed down enough and to have cultivated being open up enough to access something that will provide this embodied experience that could potentially shift our awareness. In order to keep up and produce at rates that the current, crumbling meta-paradigm demands, people's focus is mostly on the externalized world. The last thing people on this hamster wheel think is that they have the time to slow down and Observe their minds. This is survival-based living, not thriving. And I know this has been repeated because it is so nuanced that the mind typically misses it the first go around because it's such the status quo. We're about to move into something new, now, having built this foundation firmly.

One more thing: It's interesting to note and totally relevant here that when Googling the word "prana," the first page on Google returns commercial ventures with the name "prana," like yoga bags and clothing lines.

Some may say, "Good, the two worlds are beginning to meet, the mundane and the sacred."

And it's good that yoga is growing so much.

Many who believe in conspiracy theories say this is the nature of the design, to keep folks focused on what they're producing and gaining materialistically that they can then point to and others can look at and use as a measure of success for their own productivity and achievement. This seems to create people and society geared more toward physical survival. On Maslow's self-actualization hierarchy, this is the lowest level. In the yogic world, this cultural milieu leaves someone more engaged in the physical world and their physical five senses tuned into survival-based tasks. This is also considered the lowest rung on the steps toward enlightenment in the yogic world, as it is all part of the root chakra's domain. And if you're reading this, it is likely not something new for you to be considering.

The term *samsara* in Sanskrit translates into English as *that which flows together*, with the root "sam" meaning "to flow." The implied and contextualized meaning for samsara is the learning process that happens through worldly experience until wisdom is awakened to the reality beyond the physical manifestations that our physically geared five senses pick up. Samsara may also be thought of as the matrix of illusion, or *maya*, or the root error (*avidya*) of perceiving the ego-personality as who one is, rather than the indivisible pure Being-Consciousness—who one really is. And this sustains the karmic condition perceived as limitation. This cycle is considered to be the primary cause of suffering, or *duhkha*, in the yogic world.

I have just used yogic terms to describe the way we have been brought up to be in the States and in the West by our mainstream meta-paradigm—trapped in the illusion of limitation, which is the primary cause of suffering. I highly recommend pausing, breathing, rereading that last paragraph, and taking another breath.

And now, moving on.

The yogic path works with one's ego-mind and becomes more the Observer of the thoughts and beliefs and then the choices and behaviors it produces. This allows for increasing detachment to that level of existence locked into the ego-personality perceiving life through the physical five senses only, limited by and within the physically, outwardly manifested world. Gradually seeing that we are not our thoughts, nor the thinking mind, nor the ego-mind, nor the identity-based personality, is inherent to this detachment from our personality, or false identity. The ego-mind and its subconscious and unconscious blocks create in us a belief that we are that which everyone else around us also believes we are, and this further reinforces the hidden blocks. It also locks even more strongly into place the personality or ego-based identity for everyone.

Yet once we open up space for new choices to be made, there is a gradual evolving into seeing our ego-identity more from this Observer, or the Higher Self, right?

This opening allows us to come off the hamster wheel of that limited system that is locked into the physical only. It creates the ability to see through and beyond the illusion of life being only what we experience and see in our physical world that our five senses pick up on, the *maya*. The Observer is linked to the Higher Self, or the more awakened states of consciousness, not unconsciousness nor subconscious—buried— thinking and beliefs. Therefore, when people say they are seeking to be more aligned with their authentic selves, this is what they mean. They're desiring to live life from beyond the limits of the personality level, ego-mind, which is identity-based. It is their Higher Self they're seeking connection with that yields those feelings of authenticity through its alignment with something higher or bigger than the personality self. Their aligned self is aligned with this higher aspect of themselves and all of life. Another way to say this is they are aligned with the more conscious parts of themselves and all of life. Still another way to say this is that they have accessed their prana, or chi, and of all life all around them.

Again, I want to emphasize, *yoga*, in its truest definition, literally translates from Sanskrit into English as *to yoke with*.

What is it being yoked with?

All that was just described. This is the gradual awakening of a more conscious person.

The process of enlightenment is described as this realization of *samsara* as the fundamental illusion, that then leads to the transcendence of the space-time continuum that veils consciousness in layers, and consequently, reveals the true nature of self, which is inherently free. This means free to choose what it is that will make us feel freer in our lives, while all aspects of our lives are, in fact, thriving. Not where one aspect or three—say, family, more than enough material goods, and feeling centered in one's Higher Self with a good strong spiritual connection realized—are sacrificed so that thriving happens only at one level, say materialistically.

This process of awakening we have been talking about does indeed share some aspects with the process of enlightenment. We have more vital life force as we become awakened because there is more stuck unconsciousness and subconsciousness that are now released, which means more consciousness is overall available. This also creates a system that is awakened and allowed to flow out into all parts of our existence the vital life force energy—so all is enlivened. We are not just talking about the body. Remember, each chakra has a specific domain of life, mentally, emotionally, and spiritually, that it is connected to *within the physical body* — although technically the chakras aren't considered physical, which is getting too advanced for our purposes here.

This is the level of a juiced up, co-created life consciously chosen and co-created with this force of love, or satyagraha, or chi, or prana. We are full of awake, vital life force energy and consciously making choices for the highest benefit of our mind-body-spirit overall, including all levels of life that are sectioned off within each chakra. For example, the root chakra is awakened because any unconscious and subconscious blocks around survival and money have been unwound or cleared. A healthy, opened root chakra contains a feeling like we are wanted rather than feelings of being unwanted and even abandoned, and a desire to be in our bodies and lives rather than spacing out and checking out to just get by in the life we've settled for, in order to have our material lives thriving. We are actively able to move beyond just focusing on having our material levels that we desire to live at met. And our third chakra is awakened so that we feel like we have the right to desire what we desire—and we go for it, no matter what those around us may be saying in protest. And our crown chakras are opened to our Higher Self and the wisdom pouring in there. Our sixth chakras are able to listen and discern our intuitive guidance to help us see what is our own unique brilliance. We can actively, courageously make the choices required for living a life that creates those choices, coming from our own unique brilliance. The fifth chakra is open and flowing vital life force energy to the neck, throat, and thyroid, and empowering increasingly creative choices along with the courage to make these choices to create this life we're guided to create.

You are seeing this more now, yes?

Again, the way this world of consciousness works is there are layers of consciousness that are progressively revealed, the more we continue unraveling the false, identity-based self, and awaken to our eternal being, our Higher Self, present and guiding our life. It's not so mystical. It's practical and systematic as to how to go about thriving in mind, body, and spirit—and all of life. There has been much repetition here due to these layers of consciousness, as well as the requirement that some of this be experienced before we can conceptually grasp the next unveiling layer of consciousness.

The idea of the sacred sound and Sanskrit word OM has been considered to be the sound of creation, of the big bang. And within OM are vibrations that I use when teaching my Vibrational UPgrade yoga and meditation class, which help attune my students' sense of spirituality and connection to that Higher, or eternal, part of themselves and life. If you have ever been to my class or in a class — or kirtan chanting, temple, hall, or stadium — where there is a group toning OM, you are reminded that there is something beyond this chattering mind and ego with its personality and its likes and dislikes. In fact, it is much like an attunement that reminds one what is real and lasting, and what is not.

Try it: OMMMMM, have it come from the back of your throat. Or go to YouTube and listen to others chanting it, and chant along. You'll feel it and see. As with all of this stuff, it has to be experienced to be understood. And then the other possibilities become more alive.

Within this word OM, or the symbol of OM, is a highly functional guide to restore the sacred to life, and reconnect consciously with the life force that animates all life. From the *Mandakuya Upanishad* of the ancient sacred texts of India is an explanation of the Sanskrit word OM's meaning and the symbol's complete explanation. OM has also been represented in English from Sanskrit as the letters AUM.

But before we can go there, we need to go here: there is a concept within the yogic tradition of the fourth state of consciousness, that of *turiya*. This state of consciousness is beyond the waking, dreaming, or dreamless state. It is where our superconsciousness is. But it's not a state, though. Rather, turiya is infusing it all, behind it all. Turiya is the backdrop, or underlying aspect of it all, that makes the impossible seem possible. It has no limitation whatsoever.

Does this sound like a loving force?

Or, put differently, does it sound or feel like loving, parental figures wanting their children to know they can be anything they want to be, and with ease, health, and well-being?

Maybe there is something to this backdrop of all life—meaning also the backdrop within which our vital life force energy exists—being the force of love that animates all life.

Are you ready?

Here we go: turiya is represented by OM, or AUM. I'm going to give you a minute with that. And the teacher in me wants to suggest that perhaps you go back and reread the previous three paragraphs to help those words reach you more, providing the shift that this realization offers.

Each of the three arcs within the OM symbol—the three arcs on the left hand side that make it seem like it looks like the number 3—are representative of the three states of consciousness before turiya, which again is the fourth. Turiya is the one state of consciousness that the masses are the least familiar with.

The three states of consciousness that we are most familiar with are:

- First arc — represents the **waking** state, associated with *vishvanara*

- Second arc — represents the **dream** state, associated with *taijasa*

- Third arc — represents the **dreamless** state, associated with *prajna*

The dot at the very top of the OM symbol represents the third eye, located at the sixth chakra. Going deeper into this territory of consciousness that the third eye grants us access to, it represents turiya, which again is a constant, not a state. Notice how this is at the top of the entire symbol, as if exerting influence over and behind the entire encapsulation of the three most typical states of consciousness the average person is aware they're are residing in, and most familiar with: waking, dreaming, and dreamless.

The upward curve underneath the dot at the very top, as if a smile, represents *maya*, the illusion that within the yogic world and meditation world is regarded as where the typical physical, or three-dimensional world resides. The average person operating at the level of consciousness of the ego-mind, or personality level, is aware of being able to have dreams, be awake, and then go into that dreamless state. Maya is the illusion that this physical existence is what is the most real. Notice the implications that has about what science in the West has spent three centuries studying, and what we in the West elevate to the primary aspect of existence, particularly because we can touch, taste, see, feel, or smell it—or measure it more easily.

And well beyond that, maya is also considered to be responsible for the functions of creation, preservation, and dissolution of our entire existence. This fits in quite succinctly with the yogic belief that OM is the sound of creation, and what started the universe. It only makes sense that this is represented in the symbol communicating this significance, with all parts contributing to the whole.

Though invisible, AUM, or OM, has three sounds. As the sound of creation, we're not just talking about the Big Bang. We're also talking about the multiple times a day we choose something and by default *not* choose the other thing involved in that choice (e.g., getting angry with traffic or remaining detached from reacting with anger to the traffic). And a creation in our lives results.

The *A* in the AUM is *vishvanara,* and it means to not be deceived by what the senses are picking up.

The *U* in the AUM is *taijasa,* and it describes the person who is established in wisdom. This means they're not leaning into what the five senses pick up, nor what goes on in the dream state. An interesting comparison here is of a meditator meditating and cultivating the Observer, or Witness, and a dreamer dreaming; they're the same thing, comparable and coming from the same level of consciousness, within the framework of turiya, and the profound yogic wisdom that birthed it and Buddhism. I always like to remind: yoga came first, and out of yoga Buddha discovered meditation and began to teach it, which became the focus of the school of retraining the mind and then living from that space attained. So the teaching of turiya is also known within the Buddhist world.

The *M* in the AUM is *prajna,* and it is used to indicate those who know that by stilling the mind, they find their true statures and inspire everyone to grow. It sounds like Buddha lived from prajna. And within prajna is a steadiness of mind that is able to be maintained, whether in the waking or dreaming state.

People who have cultivated prajna draw you right into their aura, or field. Their energy settles you and calms you. And when people have cultivated prajna enough so that they mostly live there, then there is an aspect of removing what's in the way within the ego, and a sense of attuning that goes on when we encounter one who has cultivated prajna. This has helped me understand and make better sense of what goes on within my field as people increasingly report their blockages clearing even when I'm not consciously intending it, nor working at clearing their beliefs—or ego—with my Vibrational UPgrade energy medicine.

One woman I was chatting with for about ten minutes suddenly piped in, "Ooh! My ears just unblocked!"

I looked at this lively woman, whose company I enjoy so much, with a quizzical look on my face, so she continued. "Yes, my ears have been blocked for six months, after the last time I flew, and I've tried all these different things but nothing has worked. And now standing with you, they've become unblocked! How great is *that*?"

A smile overtook her face as I stood there witnessing this transformation.

"That's totally cool! Yeah, it seems like my field now clears people even when I'm not actively or consciously engaged in clearing or healing work. It's been fun, interesting, and a bit weird to get used to, though. Glad I could help! See how much

I love you, I don't even have to consciously intend to help, and *bam*! There it is!"

That was four years ago, and I've been continuing to notice the growing abilities of this emanation of what seems to be the state of prajna affect others' fields, even when not actively engaged in healing or clearing work.

In the waking and dream states, there is apprehension. In the dreamless state there is none, nor is there judgment. In the dreamless state there is deep rest because there is no longer the dualistic conceptualization of me and you, and no objects and perceiver of these objects.

And so it is the goal of bringing in the one from the dreamless state into the waking state, yes?

And as revealed in deep sleep, it is understood in yogic wisdom that this is the essential nature of brahman (divinity), and it is defined as *chaitanya*, which can be translated as *pure consciousness*. This pure consciousness is distinguished from prana, which is more clearly defined as *vitality*. Of the many aspects of yoga and its offerings, I know this is what I appreciate the most of what the yogic wisdom offers us in the West: an understanding of the different types of consciousness, levels, and a road map to help us realize the states that are more beneficial, while increasingly being able to detach from the ones that cause suffering. At the same time, an awareness that all of this is even possible is also greatly appreciated.

A month after first learning about this fourth state of consciousness, turiya, from Gurudev Amrit Desai at his Amrit yoga retreat, assisted by his senior teacher, Chandrakant, a.k.a., "The Revealer" (because he considers himself more a revealer than a teacher due to the nature of yoga and consciousness, or prana), I returned to see Gurudev, and gift him another energy medicine session. I found myself in such a state of profound gratitude for all that he has done to bring the teachings of yoga to the United States that I wanted to give back. You see, Gurudev Shri Amritji (Yogi Amrit Desai) is one of a handful of gurus who came to America from India in the early 1960s. This wave began the initial yoga craze that has grown into the massive and diverse yoga practices we have worldwide today. Amritji was one of the first arrivals and the last living guru from this initial wave, and a pioneer in bringing the authentic practice of yoga to the West. The methodology he developed has evolved from Kripalu yoga into Amrit yoga, as the founder of holistic yoga centers of both names. He is a traditionalist, as I am, retaining the pure form of Patanjali's sutras for yoga, with the eight limbs to be practiced and experienced, not just the one-size-fits-all yoga class so popular in America. Five of those eight limbs — my students hear me say this all the time — are about meditation; it is only one of the eight limbs that are about the asanas, or body postures.

How to move beyond one's ego-mind center, and thus allow one's I AM consciousness to take the lead is in great part the instruction one gains from Gurudev's development of the integrated Amrit yoga method, the *posture of consciousness*. The focus is on consciousness and prana, well beyond only the body postures. In fact, it's almost the last thing we get to with Gurudev, because as he presents it, all the tools he has developed are to get someone to the point of being able to tune in enough to allow the prana to move the body, rather than the mind leading this process.

This is where Gurudev got me. Because I am still seeking to understand at even more refined levels what prana or this vital life force is and can do. Yes, even after having chosen to move to

Asia and live there for ten years to study subtle energy, with my yoga teacher training and certification in traditional Ashtanga yoga in India, and practicing yoga and meditation for twenty-five years, I'm still seeking.

And personally, I was so elated to have found a teacher who was speaking to exactly the area that I wanted to know more about. It isn't often anymore that I find someone I can learn from, quite honestly. So I was full of relief at having found one who could still continue to point out smaller nuanced understandings after years of practice. Besides, I'd heard he loved bodywork.

We were in his gorgeous office, sectioned off from his gorgeous log home, with hand-carved wooden moldings everywhere, overlooking a lake. Gurudev's own brilliant artwork and bright, beaming crystals were everywhere, as were books, and what seemed to me to be imported from India — a palace style of furniture, fit for royalty. I was getting updated on his progress from his last session.

"I've been doing that pose the way you showed me and it has really helped open my hips, Alison."

"Gurudev, that was so strange for me! Me showing you, a yoga guru, a yoga pose! I was like, 'But Gurudev, you already know this! You've been teaching this for decades! You come from this practice!'"

He's a guru of this practice, after all!

Smiling quizzically at me, Gurudev happily responded, "Yes, but you showed me a different way. I can always learn more!"

Debbie, his assistant, added, "He's always reading."

Okay, I thought. This actually fits in with his energy — always open, remaining child-like. "So Gurudev, can I ask you something?"

It reminded me of the Zen concept of beginner's mind. And it reminded me of me. In fact, Gurudev was a fellow Libra. I was visiting a week after his eighty-third birthday.

"Yes," he looked down at me from his office chair, with his legs sitting in simple log stacking posture.

I was on the floor of his office because I'd been showing Debbie what pose I'd taught Gurudev to do, to help her better grasp what we were talking about.

"So you know how Gandhi called satyagraha a love force and a soul force?"

"Yes," he was smiling.

"Well, is that the same as prana?"

"Alison, you have just named three things that are all the same, just with different names."

I looked up at Gurudev with such appreciation for the simplicity and directness of his response.

"Okay," I said and stood up. "Shall we go do your session now, Gurudev?"

"Yes," he replied, smiling at me with that twinkle that seemed to bounce out of his eyes and enter into me, unfolding himself out of the chair he'd been sitting in.

And off we went, up the stairs for another co-creative harmony of me emptied, receptive, and allowing the prana to lead the way as Gurudev's system readily invited the prana into wherever it would most support the continued thriving of his masterfully cultivated mind-body system.

Conclusion

We are now learning what it means to be a conscious co-creator on our planet. Where what we desire to create is *not* out of reach.

Where the old habits of procrastination, and the general attitude of "not going for what we truly want and just settling for what others around us are doing or a bit more than that" no longer has the hold on us.

That is what this book — and my work — assist with. To move out of the not dreaming anymore as an adult, or not growing bigger the dreams, or of not welcoming the unlimited possibilities beyond what we've already created are all in action, or up for us now, depending on where we're at with unwinding our unconscious and subconscious beliefs.

There is a vast amalgam of diverse unconscious and subconscious beliefs that I am continuing to be surprised by that serve to limit what it is people allow themselves to go for with their lives and living. It becomes quite nuanced. And it's perfect, because here we are on the precipice of seeing more tangibly the effects of being in humanity's greatest leap in evolution, ever. Indeed, learning how to live as an Awakened Presence embodied within our physical bodies and create our lives at the everyday mundane level, while living immersed within and around us these sacred frequencies and vibrations to support us all in our spiritual awakening, seems to be leading us to creating more enriched lives than we ever dreamed was possible.

The vast array of subtle, nuanced beliefs from our conditioning, from the imprints our parents left us with, and all the other sources described that create our perspective that we then look out at life from on a day-to-day basis is exactly where to start.

And this does not only mean meditating or some kind of practice that causes you to look within. It also means actively making choices that before you wouldn't have allowed yourself to go for, and see then what shows up. Creation in action, as well as going within to listen, gain clarity, and create the consciousness within your field of your mind, body, and spirit that will allow for, and further catalyze, the universal life force all around you to be more activated—or directed—on your behalf by your desires and choices.

What exists at our unconscious and subconscious level seems to want the light shone on it. We're being asked—and some would even say commanded—to learn how we are in fact creating our reality through our choices. And the implication is: so we can create an even greater reality, one that is in harmony with the chi, prana, or vital life force that is all around us, and throughout all animate life, including ourselves, our systems, our chakras. This does require us to go in, both individually and collectively, to our consciousness because this is where our hidden beliefs, conclusions, and views of how the world works reside. We need to address the beliefs that are stopping us individually and collectively and causing us to create a life and planet and global community that is not contributing to the well-being of ourselves, our families, our communities, our institutions, our health and well-being, and our planet's continued—and improved—health and well-being.

Once we have in fact cleared out the bulk of our unconscious and subconscious beliefs that have caused us to create what is not in alignment, we are then, therefore, able to choose more of what will contribute to the overall well-being for all by choosing that which will create it for ourselves.

Some of us are aware that we are plugged in and wired to be more in tune with operating for not just our own lives, but at the level of the collective. Nonetheless, all of us are influencing the collective. So it behooves us to really clear out the old, dense, outdated unconsciousness. Once more of us are living within systems that are increasingly clear of the lower densities, and our choices are more aligned and attuned to the higher vibrations, the highest potential, then this upliftment becomes easier for all. And it is this exact act of upliftment, of enlightening one's system via the awakening process described within this book, that we are then more effective at creating a world that is of the higher vibrations that are the nature of our times. It is a conspiracy for our bliss, indeed! And it's not just wishful thinking.

If my system thrives from my choosing more of what will expand my life and helps me evolve into becoming more of who I am here to be, or realizing more of my potential, then is that not a conspiracy for our bliss?

In fact, what I have seen causing most people's struggles is the holding on of what does not evolve us. And this is the crux of where we are on our planet now, individually and collectively. This work is not just personal; it is political and global.

It is completely within our power to learn how to, with increasing ease and comfort and adeptness, choose *for* ourselves, our lives, our living, our communities, our planet and less choosing *against* all that we desire. For many of us, we've spent the past few years clearing out the blocks to being more able to go for what it is we desire, and where we've sabotaged our own thriving, through the type of clearings and activations suggested in the "Next Steps" section that follows.

Next Steps

Sign up to receive ongoing bi-weekly support via our inspirational newsletters and then sample the Vibrational UPgrade for yourself with the monthly free call, where you can gain free one-on-one facilitation during this high-spirited group call. You'll receive a free MP3, *Clearing the Most Frequent Blocks to Success*. Visit www.alisonjkay.com.

Everyone can benefit from the *Chakra Attunement Audio Series*. If you're new to working with having your energy — or consciousness — cleared, then start with listening daily to the MP3 for one chakra. If you're not new to this clearing of the unconscious and subconscious blocks within each chakra, then you can handle two a day, at most. Please give yourself a month of listening — at least once a day and at most five times a week, before you take the next step after that — which is to reach out to me so I can supercharge your field, boosting your results from working in a one-on-one capacity, whether in person or from distance. You can find the *Chakra Attunement Audio Series* at www.alisonjkay.com/chakra-healing-audio-series/.

If you see yourself really needing strengthening around not allowing your ego-mind to continue to make excuses that cause you to pay more attention to the doubt-ridden list of "Why not to go for it" instead of your heart's inspiration and therefore calling to Yes, go for it, then purchase the three MP3 product, *Stop Stopping Yourself!* These are full-on, gentle-yet-fierce clearings, activations, and downloads that have the cumulative effect of opening up your Co-Creator's Channel with the relevant frequencies so that your new vibration — and new life — await you. These programs gently provide access to the Higher, Eternal parts of you and your innate guidance system so you stay aligned and inspired, rather than shrinking back and stagnant. This is a perfect accompanying body of work for this book's content in which to deepen, enrich, and activate within you the physical actualization of these concepts showing up in you, your inner dialogue, your choices, and thus your life.

If you're already advanced and have been actively working with your co-creative abilities, then hop onto the Tuesday night group call ASAP! This group call continues to gain in momentum and potency with the vibrations of firmly bringing forth your co-creative power, while clearing out wherever you're continuing to unconsciously sabotage your own efforts to create all that you desire.

If you're super-ready and it's a really strong Yes! for a quantum leap, then contact Dr. Alison to begin a transformation series of one-on-one sessions.

Visit www.alisonjkay.com/one-on-one-sessions/

About the Author

Dr. Alison J. Kay has worked as a Master Mind-Body Energy Medicine practitioner for more than twenty years. A world-traveler who lived and worked at an International School in Asia for ten years, she currently facilitates energy healings for clients worldwide.

During her experience in Asia, Alison completed her PhD as a Holistic Life Coach. She continued fiercely studying Buddhism and Buddhist meditation, while also learning and eventually teaching chi gong, and receiving traditional Chinese and other Asian holistic treatments many times per week. Prior to returning home, Dr. Alison went to India and became a Yoga Alliance certified yoga and meditation teacher. She created the Vibrational UPgrade System after spending these years in Asia studying subtle energy. Her system presents the intersection of the mind, body, and spirit applied to cultivating vitality, health, longevity, and overall well-being. During her speaking engagements, she consistently awes her audiences with the completeness and accuracy from which they awaken and recognize their own physical, emotional, mental, and life challenges having a direct, clear correlation to a specific chakra or two. She has developed a system that targets the missing links that have been understood to be the weak points in the American medical system of daily self and chronic care, as she fully documents in her well-researched first book, *What if There's Nothing Wrong?* released in 2013.

Dr. Alison also presents holistic tools to transform long-term issues that take students and clients beyond wellness into levels of thriving not typically expected nor considered possible within the American system.

Dr. Alison uncovers the unifying tools with the understanding of how energy flows — or does not — in the body, and how that creates:

- Health and wellness
- Vitality and clarity
- Centered calmness
- Abundance
- Healthy emotional expression
- Balance and a whole lot more
- Vibrant career paths based on passion, alignment, and fulfillment
- Healthy expressions of love: giving, receiving, romantic, family, friends, self
- Physical flexibility, ease, and longevity

Accreditations and Certifications

- BA, Bachelors of Arts in English literature with creative writing minor
- MPA, Masters of Public Administration
- PhD, Doctor of Philosophy as a Holistic Life Coach
- Holistic health practitioner with the American Holistic Health Association, AHHA
- Usui Shiki Ryoho Reiki Master lineage to the founder, removed by six
- Level 5 Certification, Masters Level, for the Tibetan Energy Medicine Adamantine Healing System (AHS)
- Basic and Advanced Certified ThetaHealing™ Practitioner
- BARS practitioner with Access Consciousness™
- India-trained Ashtanga yoga teacher
- Yoga Alliance registered yoga teacher of 200 hours (RYT-200)
- Qigong instructor
- Buddhist meditation practitioner for twenty-three years
- Buddhist meditation teacher with signature talk, "The Nature of the Mind" for twenty-two years
- ACE-certified personal trainer with certification in fitness and longevity nutrition

Dr. Alison's business has won many awards, including the local County Advisory Board's "Creating Pinellas," an unexpected prize declaring Dr. Alison's business as a contribution to Pinellas county, the second-largest county in Florida, and its residents. The successes Dr. Alison's clients have experienced in working with her have earned her the title of Number One Energy Healer on Thumbtack's app for two consecutive years. Recognition for Dr. Alison's first book, *What if There's Nothing Wrong?* includes being awarded one of the top-twelve Most Spirited Female-Authored Books.

Dr. Alison currently resides in Florida specializing in mind-body fitness. She holds a specialized certification in for fitness and longevity nutrition.

For more information about products and services available, visit her website at www.AlisonJKay.com.

www.ingramcontent.com/pod-product-compliance
Lightning Source LLC
Chambersburg PA
CBHW071912290426
44110CB00013B/1366